Hidden No More. Personal & Small Group Study Guide

The Secrets God Reveals

Dr. Mike Prah

Mpaebo Media

Published by Mpaebo Media a division of Mike Prah, LLC, Severn, MD. www.mikeprah.com

Scripture quotations are from the following sources:

The Holy Bible, New International Version (NIV). Copyright © 1973, 1978, 1984, 2011 by Biblica, Inc.™. Used by permission. All rights reserved.

Scripture quotations marked LB are taken from The Living Bible, Copyright © 1971 by Tyndale House Foundation. Used by permission of Tyndale House Publishers, Inc., Carol Stream, Illinois 60188. All rights reserved.

Italics in Scripture reflect the author's added emphasis.

U. S. Library of Congress Cataloging-in-Publication Data

Prah, Mike, Author

Hidden no more. personal & small group study guide : the secrets God reveals / Mike Prah.

First Edition, 2026.

Severn, Maryland : Mpaebo Media, 2026 | Includes Scripture references, discussion questions, personal reflection guides, and daily believer declarations.

pages cm

ISBN 978-1-969340-14-7 (paperback)

ISBN 978-1-969340-15-4 (ebook)

Subjects: LCSH: Christian life—Study and teaching | Christian life—Biblical teaching | Spiritual formation—Christianity | Discipleship—Christianity | Bible—Study and teaching.

Classification: BV4501.3.P73 2026 | DDC 248.4—dc23

LCCN: 1-15135800192

Printed in the United States of America

Special Bulk Discounts and Custom Editions:

Most books authored by Mike Prah are available at special discounted rates for bulk purchases by churches, organizations, businesses, and individuals. Customized editions or book excerpts can also be created to meet the specific needs of your ministry, event, or audience. For more information or to inquire about a special order, please contact: info@mikeprah.com. Available through major U.S. and international online book retailers. Signed copies are also available from the author.

Direct purchases are available at http://mikeprah.com/bookstore

Mystērion

"The mystery that has been kept hidden for ages and generations is now disclosed to the Lord's people."

— Colossians 1:26 (NIV)

What God once concealed in His redemptive plan has now been revealed through Jesus Christ.

Welcome Letter

Dear Friend,

Grace and peace to you.

It is my joy to welcome you to the *Hidden No More: Secrets God Reveals — Personal & Small Group Study Guide*. Whether you are walking through this material on your own or with others, you are stepping into an intentional journey of spiritual growth, biblical reflection, and Christ-centered transformation.

This guide was designed to do more than simply review information from the book. It was created to help you engage Scripture personally, think deeply, pray honestly, and respond practically to what God is revealing.

While this study guide is designed to work alongside the main *Hidden No More: Secrets God Reveals* book, it has also been written in such a way that individuals and groups can still benefit meaningfully even if they have not yet read the full book. Each session contains biblical teaching, Scripture discovery, reflection, discussion, application, and prayer designed to help participants understand and live out the truths being explored.

At the same time, I strongly encourage you to read the main book whenever possible. The book provides the larger teaching framework, fuller theological development, illustrations, and pastoral insights that enrich and deepen the study experience.

You will also find Daily Believer Declarations throughout the study experience. These declarations are designed to help reinforce biblical truth, renew your thinking, strengthen your faith, and keep your heart anchored in God's promises throughout the week. Each declaration combines Scripture, faith-filled confession, and prayer to help move truth from the page into daily life.

Rather than allowing truth to remain only intellectual, the Daily Believer Declarations are intended to help cultivate ongoing spiritual formation — shaping identity, strengthening hope, encouraging dependence on God, and helping believers walk intentionally in what God is revealing.

Each chapter of this guide invites you to slow down and engage God's truth intentionally. The goal is not simply to finish material, but to create space for the Holy Spirit to shape your thinking, deepen your faith, and strengthen your walk with God.

If you are using this guide in a group, my encouragement is simple: be honest, be gracious, and be expectant. God often works powerfully in environments where people are willing to listen, learn, share, and grow together.

If you are using this guide personally, take your time. There is no need to rush. Spiritual growth is not built on speed, but on steady surrender and consistent responsiveness to God.

My prayer for you is this:

That what God has revealed would not remain hidden in your life, That His truth would take deep root in your heart, And that His presence would steadily shape you from the inside out.

You are not walking this journey alone. God is with you, and He delights in revealing Himself to those who seek Him.

With gratitude and expectation,

Mike Prah

Contents

INTRODUCTION

There is a difference between knowing truth and living from it.

Many believers sincerely desire to grow. We read Scripture, we listen, we learn—and yet we often find ourselves asking a deeper question:

How does this truth actually change my life?

That is where this guide comes in.

The purpose of this companion is not simply to help you review information, but to help you engage, internalize, and live out what God has revealed. Each chapter is designed to move you from understanding to transformation through Scripture, reflection, discussion, application, and prayer.

God reveals truth not to impress us, but to draw us closer to Himself, guide our lives, transform our hearts, and strengthen us for every season we face. As you journey through this guide, you will begin to discover that what was once hidden is now being made visible—not only in Scripture, but also in your everyday life.

This journey is not about perfection. It is about relationship.

It is not about striving harder. It is about responding to what God is already doing.

It is not about having all the answers. It is about walking closely with the One who does.

And as you do, something begins to change.

As you move through this guide, you may sense moments where God is drawing your heart closer—inviting you to trust Him more deeply, surrender more fully, or begin a relationship with Him in a new way.

If that is where you find yourself, you can respond right where you are by praying this simple prayer:

Father God, I come to You with an open heart. I acknowledge my need for You and my desire to know You more deeply. I place my trust in Jesus Christ—His life, His death, and His resurrection. Forgive me, renew me, and make me new. Teach me to walk with You and to live from the life You have placed within me. I receive Your grace and surrender my life to You. In Jesus' name, Amen.

God is not distant from you. He is near—and He is already at work.

The secrets to a fulfilled and faithful life are no longer hidden. Through Scripture, God reveals truth to bring clarity, inspire transformation, strengthen hope, and lead you more deeply into the life He has redeemed for you.

How To Use This Guide

This study guide is designed to be flexible, Scripture-centered, discussion-friendly, and spiritually practical.

Whether you are using it personally, with a small group, in a discipleship setting, or in a church environment, the goal is not simply to complete lessons, but to help God's truth move from information into transformation.

Each chapter is built around a simple discipleship flow:

1. Read

2. Reflect

3. Discuss

4. Apply

5. Pray

The structure is designed to help participants engage Scripture personally, process truth honestly, and respond practically.

A Note About the Main Book

This guide was created to accompany the Hidden No More: The Secrets

God Reveals book series, and reading the corresponding book chapters is strongly encouraged whenever possible.

The main book provides:

• Deeper biblical teaching,

• Fuller theological explanation,

• Illustrations and practical insight,

• Pastoral reflection, and

• Broader context for each theme.

However, this guide has also been intentionally written so that individuals and groups who have not yet read the full book can still participate meaningfully and benefit spiritually from the teaching.

Each session includes:

• A chapter overview,

• Scripture-centered discussion,

• Biblical insights,

• Reflection questions,

• Application prompts,

• Prayer points, and

• Key truths to remember.

This means groups may use the study guide on its own if necessary, though the richest experience will come from engaging both the book and the guide together.

For Personal Use

• Set aside intentional time each week for one chapter.

- Begin with prayer and ask the Holy Spirit for understanding.

- Read the corresponding chapter from the main book if available.

- Work through the study guide slowly and honestly.

- Take time to reflect before moving quickly to answers.

- Write down personal insights, prayers, or Scriptures that stand out.

- Use the Key Truth to Remember and Daily Believer Declarations throughout the week.

- Read the declarations slowly and prayerfully.

- Speak them aloud when possible.

- Allow the Scriptures and prayers to shape your thinking and strengthen your faith daily.

- Return to them during moments of discouragement, anxiety, uncertainty, or spiritual weariness.

Remember: this is not about rushing through content. It is about walking steadily with God.

For Small Groups

Recommended Group Flow

1. Welcome and Opening Prayer

2. Icebreaker Discussion

3. Chapter Review & Personal Reflection

4. Scripture Discovery (main discussion section)

5. Application & Reflection

6. Group Prayer

Group Discussion Tips

• Spend most of your time in the Scripture Discovery section.

• Encourage participation, not perfection.

• Allow people to process honestly without pressure.

• Keep bringing discussion back to the Scripture text.

• Avoid rushing silence; reflection often leads to deeper insight.

• Focus on spiritual formation, not merely completing material.

Leader Encouragement

You do not need to have all the answers to lead effectively. Your role is not to perform, but to help create space for people to encounter God's truth together.

Listen well. Guide gently. Keep Christ and Scripture central. Trust the Holy Spirit to work.

Helpful Tips for Small Group Leaders

Leading a small group is more than facilitating discussion—it is creating space for people to encounter God's truth, grow in community, and take meaningful steps in their walk with Christ. Whether you are leading one session or an entire series, remember that you do not have to lead perfectly. God delights in using willing, prayerful, and faithful leaders. As you serve others, trust that the Holy Spirit will guide, strengthen, and work through you along the way.

1. Be Authentic and Welcoming

Be yourself—God intends to use your unique personality and gifts. Greet each person warmly as they arrive. A genuine smile and kind welcome can set the tone for the entire gathering. Remember, showing up may have taken courage for some. Create an environment where people feel seen, valued, and safe.

Don't feel pressure to have all the answers. If you're unsure, simply say so. If you make a mistake, own it graciously. Authenticity builds trust and fosters meaningful connection.

2. Prepare with Purpose

Take time before each meeting to review the discussion material. Reflect on the questions and consider your own responses. Most sessions include more content than can be covered in one meeting—prayerfully select the questions that best serve your group's needs. Preparation allows you to lead with confidence and clarity.

3. Facilitate, Don't Dominate

Small groups thrive on discussion, not lectures. Ask questions and allow space for responses. Silence is not your enemy—it often means people are thinking. Resist the urge to fill every pause or "preach" after each answer.

Affirm contributions with simple encouragement like, *"Thank you for sharing,"* or *"That's a great insight."* Then invite others in: *"Would anyone else like to add?"* Create space for every voice.

4. Guide the Flow with Grace

Provide smooth transitions between questions and sections. Invite volunteers to read Scripture or discussion prompts rather than calling on individuals directly.

If one person tends to dominate, gently redirect the conversation:

"Let's hear from someone who hasn't shared yet."

Your goal is to cultivate balanced participation where everyone feels included.

5. Cover Your Group in Prayer

Prayer is the foundation of every effective group. Begin by praying for your members by name. Ask God to guide your time and speak to each heart.

When needs arise during the meeting, pause and pray together. Stay sensitive to the leading of the Holy Spirit. Prayer transforms the atmosphere and deepens spiritual connection.

6. Share the Leadership

You don't have to carry the responsibility alone. Consider inviting a co-leader or rotating facilitation roles. Jesus sent His disciples out in pairs (Luke 10:1), modeling shared ministry.

This not only lightens your load but also strengthens the group by developing others.

7. Honor Time and Commitment

Respect the schedules of your group members. Start and end on time whenever possible. Clear expectations build trust and encourage consistency.

8. Cultivate Joy and Connection

Create a warm, engaging, and enjoyable environment. Laugh together. Celebrate moments. Allow relationships to grow naturally.

Scripture reminds us, *"A cheerful heart is good medicine"* (Proverbs 17:22, NIV). Don't be overly rigid—leave room for genuine connection and Spirit-led moments.

A Shepherd's Heart: Prepare Spiritually

Before leading your first session, take time to prayerfully reflect on these Scriptures. Ask God to shape your heart as a shepherd who leads with compassion, humility, and love:

• Matthew 9:36–38

• John 10:14–15

• 1 Peter 5:2–4

• Philippians 2:1–5

• Hebrews 10:23–25

• 1 Thessalonians 2:7–8, 11–12

Let these passages anchor your leadership in Christ's example. As you lead, remember: you are not just guiding a discussion—you are shepherding people God deeply loves.

Chapter 1 Study Guide: Why God Reveals Secrets

A. SESSION AIM

To help participants understand that God reveals truth not to impress us, but to draw us into relationship with Him, guide them in wisdom, transform them from the inside out, and strengthen them to endure life's challenges with faith and hope.

B. ICE BREAKER

What is something you once misunderstood that later became clear—and changed the way you lived or responded?

Leader Note: Keep the atmosphere relaxed and conversational. Encourage participants to share simple personal experiences that highlight how clarity often changes behavior and perspective.

C. OPEN YOUR SESSION WITH PRAYER

Invite someone to open in prayer, or use the prayer below:

Heavenly Father, thank You for being a God who reveals truth. Open our hearts and minds today to understand Your Word more deeply. Help us not only to hear Your truth, but to respond to it with humility, faith, and obedience. Draw us closer to You through this discussion and let Your

Spirit transform us from the inside out. In Jesus' name, Amen.

D. INTRODUCTION (CHAPTER 1 SUMMARY)

Many people spend their lives searching for meaning, direction, and clarity. Deep within the human heart is a longing to understand what is hidden—to know why we are here, what God desires, and how we should live. Yet Scripture teaches that the deepest truths of life are not discovered merely through intelligence, effort, or experience. They are revealed by God.

The Bible presents God not as distant or unwilling to speak, but as a loving Father who delights in revealing truth to His people. God reveals truth so we can know Him more deeply, walk wisely, experience transformation, and endure life's hardships with hope. Revelation is not merely about gaining information—it is about entering into relationship with God and allowing His truth to shape our lives.

In this session, we will explore five important reasons God reveals truth and how His revelation changes the way we think, live, and follow Him.

E. BIBLE DISCUSSION

SECTION 1: PERSONALIZING THE MESSAGE

1. Have you ever experienced a moment when God brought clarity or understanding to something you were struggling with?

2. Why do you think people often look for answers apart from God?

3. In what areas of life do you most desire God's wisdom and direction right now?

4. What does it mean to you personally that God desires to reveal truth to His people?

SECTION 2: SCRIPTURE DISCOVERY

KEY POINT 1: God Reveals Truth to Those Who Humbly Seek Him

Scriptures: Matthew 11:25–26; James 4:8

Scripture Insights: God's truth is not primarily revealed through pride, self-sufficiency, or intellectual achievement. Jesus taught that spiritual understanding is given to those who approach God with humility, openness, and childlike dependence. Revelation flows through relationship and surrender. As believers draw near to God, He graciously makes His truth known and brings clarity to their hearts and minds.

Discussion Questions:

1. Read Matthew 11:25–26. Why did Jesus say truth was hidden from the "wise and learned" but revealed to "little children"?

2. What attitudes or mindsets can make people resistant to God's truth?

3. Read James 4:8. What promise does God give to those who draw near to Him?

4. How does humility help us grow spiritually?

5. What is one practical way you can draw closer to God this week?

KEY POINT 2: God Reveals Truth Through Relationship

Scriptures: John 15:15; Psalm 25:14; Ephesians 1:17

Scripture Insights:

God does not reveal truth merely to inform us—He reveals truth to invite us into deeper relationship with Him. Jesus called His disciples friends because He made known to them what the Father revealed to Him. Revelation is relational before it is informational. The closer we walk with God, the clearer His truth becomes.

Discussion Questions:

1. Read John 15:15. What is the difference between a servant and a friend according to Jesus?

2. Read Psalm 25:14. What does it mean that "the Lord confides" in those who fear Him?

3. Why is relationship with God essential for spiritual understanding?

4. How does revelation deepen our intimacy with God?

5. What habits help cultivate closeness with God consistently?

KEY POINT 3: God Reveals Truth to Guide Us in Wisdom and Direction

Scriptures: 1 Corinthians 2:10–12; Psalm 32:8; Romans 12:1–2

Scripture Insights: God reveals truth because He cares about how His people live and the direction they take. Through the Holy Spirit, believers receive wisdom, discernment, and guidance for life. God's direction is not mechanical or distant—it is personal and relational. As our minds are renewed through His Word, we gain greater clarity for wise decisions and faithful living.

Discussion Questions:

1. Read 1 Corinthians 2:10–12. What role does the Holy Spirit play in understanding God's truth?

2. Why is human wisdom alone insufficient for discerning God's will?

3. Read Psalm 32:8. What does this verse reveal about God's heart toward His people?

4. According to Romans 12:1–2, how does transformation help believers discern God's will?

5. In what area of your life do you need God's wisdom and guidance most right now?

KEY POINT 4: God Reveals Truth to Transform Us from the Inside Out

Scriptures: 2 Corinthians 3:18; Ephesians 4:22–24; Colossians 3:9–10

Scripture Insights: God's truth was never meant to remain mere information. Revelation leads to transformation. As believers behold Christ and allow God's truth to renew their minds, the Holy Spirit gradually reshapes their desires, attitudes, identity, and character. Transformation is not instant perfection—it is an ongoing process of becoming more like Christ.

Discussion Questions:

1. Read 2 Corinthians 3:18. What does Paul mean when he says believers are "being transformed"?

2. Why is spiritual transformation usually a gradual process rather than an instant change?

3. According to Ephesians 4:22–24, what are the three movements involved in transformation?

4. How does renewing the mind affect everyday behavior and decisions?

5. What is one area where God may currently be transforming your thinking or character?

KEY POINT 5: God Reveals Truth to Strengthen Us for Endurance

Scriptures: Colossians 1:24–29; 2 Corinthians 4:16–18

Scripture Insights: God's revelation not only guides and transforms believers—it also strengthens them during seasons of suffering and hardship. Scripture teaches that Christ's presence within us provides endurance, hope, and inward renewal even when outward circumstances are difficult. Revelation gives suffering meaning and helps believers maintain an eternal perspective during trials.

Discussion Questions:

1. Read Colossians 1:27. What does "Christ in you, the hope of glory" mean to you personally?

2. Why is it important to understand that suffering is not always a sign of spiritual failure?

3. Read 2 Corinthians 4:16–18. How does Paul contrast outward suffering with inward renewal?

4. How does focusing on eternal truth help believers endure temporary hardships?

5. What truth from God's Word has helped strengthen you during difficult seasons?

F. SECTION 3: PERSONAL APPLICATION & REFLECTION

1. Which reason God reveals truth speaks most strongly to your current season of life?

2. What truth has God already revealed to you that you may need to obey more fully?

3. In what area do you need spiritual transformation or renewed thinking?

4. What practical step can you take this week to grow closer to God and become more attentive to His voice?

G. CLOSING WISDOM KEYS

God reveals truth not merely to inform us, but to draw us into deeper relationship with Him.

Revelation becomes transformational when we respond with humility, faith, and obedience.

God's truth guides us wisely, renews us inwardly, and strengthens us to endure faithfully.

H. PRAYER

I. PRAYER POINTS

1. Ask God to give you a humble and teachable heart that is open to His truth.

2. Pray for wisdom, discernment, and greater sensitivity to the Holy Spirit's guidance.

3. Present your personal needs before God and ask Him for strength, clarity, and direction.

4. Ask the Holy Spirit to continue transforming your mind, renewing your heart, and strengthening your faith.

Ask for individual prayer requests and pray for the individual needs of your group members and any area the Spirit directs.

II. CLOSING PRAYER

Heavenly Father, thank You for being a God who reveals truth to Your people. Thank You for not leaving us in darkness, confusion, or uncertainty. Draw us closer to You and help us walk in humility, wisdom, and obedience. Renew our minds through Your Word and transform our hearts through Your Spirit. Strengthen us during difficult seasons and help us live faithfully in the light of what You have revealed. May our lives increasingly reflect Christ in all we do. In Jesus' name, Amen.

Use the Chapter 1 Daily Believer Declarations during the week.

KEY TRUTH TO REMEMBER

God reveals truth not to impress us, but to draw us closer, guide our lives, transform our hearts, and strengthen us to endure.

DAILY BELIEVER DECLARATIONS (CHAPTER 1)

Why God Reveals Secrets

Day 1 — Relationship

Scripture: James 4:8; Psalm 25:14

Declaration: I draw near to God, and He draws near to me. God desires relationship with me, and He reveals His truth as I walk closely with Him.

Prayer: Lord Jesus, I choose to walk closely with You today. Open my heart to know You more deeply and help me remain attentive to Your presence. In Your name. Amen.

Day 2 — Wisdom

Scripture: 1 Corinthians 2:10–12; Proverbs 3:5–6

Declaration: God guides my life with wisdom. Through His Spirit, I receive insight and understanding for every decision I face.

Prayer: Holy Spirit, guide my thoughts and decisions today. Help me trust Your wisdom above my own understanding. In Jesus' name. Amen.

Day 3 — God's Will

Scripture: Romans 12:1–2; Colossians 1:9

Declaration: As my mind is renewed by God's Word, His will becomes clearer to me. I surrender my plans and trust God to lead me step by step.

Prayer: Father, I offer my life to You today. Renew my mind and align my heart with Your will. In Jesus' name. In Jesus' name. Amen.

Day 4 — Transformation

Scripture: 2 Corinthians 3:18; Ephesians 4:22–24

Declaration: God's truth is transforming me from the inside out. I am being renewed in my thinking and formed into the image of Christ.

Prayer: Lord, continue Your work of transformation in me. Renew my mind and shape my life according to Your truth. In Jesus' name. Amen.

Day 5 — Growth

Scripture: Philippians 1:6; Colossians 3:10

Declaration: My spiritual growth is progressive and purposeful. God is faithfully working in me through every season of my life.

Prayer: Thank You, God, for Your patience and faithfulness. Help me trust Your process and grow steadily in You. In Jesus' name. Amen.

Day 6 — Endurance

Scripture: 2 Corinthians 4:16–18; Colossians 1:29

Declaration: When life is hard, God strengthens me inwardly. His truth anchors my faith and gives me strength to endure with hope.

Prayer: Lord, strengthen me where I feel weak today. Help me fix my eyes on what is eternal and not lose heart. In Jesus' name. Amen.

Day 7 — Thanksgiving & Praise

Scripture: Psalm 103:1–5; Colossians 1:12

Declaration: I thank God for revealing His truth in my life. I praise Him for walking with me, guiding me, transforming me, and sustaining me.

Prayer: Father, I thank You for Your grace and faithfulness. I praise You for all You have done and all You are doing in my life. In Jesus' name. A men.

Chapter 2 Study Guide: The Secret of the Kingdom of God

A. SESSION AIM

To help participants understand that God's Kingdom invites trust over anxiety, reshapes priorities around Christ's reign, and assures believers that God is always at work—even during seasons when His activity seems hidden.

B. ICE BREAKER

What is something in life that only works properly when it stays connected to its source—and why?

Leader Note: Encourage simple and practical answers. Help participants begin thinking about dependence, alignment, and what happens when something loses connection to its source of strength or direction.

C. OPEN YOUR SESSION WITH PRAYER

Invite someone to open in prayer, or use the prayer below:

Heavenly Father, thank You for revealing the reality of Your Kingdom through Jesus Christ. Open our hearts today to understand what it means to live under Your reign. Help us trust You more deeply, reorder our priorities according to Your truth, and remain faithful even when we cannot see what You are doing. Let Your Kingdom shape our thinking, our decisions, and our daily lives. In Jesus' name, Amen.

D. INTRODUCTION (CHAPTER 2 SUMMARY)

Many people live with the assumption that life is controlled by circumstances, uncertainty, pressure, or fear. Yet Jesus proclaimed a radically different reality: the Kingdom of God has come near. God's reign is not merely a future promise—it is a present reality breaking into ordinary life through Christ.

The Kingdom of God is not simply about religious activity or moral behavior. It is about God's rule reshaping the human heart from the inside out. Wherever God's authority is welcomed and trusted, the Kingdom is at work. Jesus taught that this Kingdom often grows quietly and gradually, yet its influence transforms lives, priorities, and perspectives.

In this session, we will explore how God's Kingdom replaces anxiety with trust, reorders our values around Christ's reign, and assures us that God is actively working even in seasons when His purposes seem hidden.

E. BIBLE DISCUSSION

SECTION 1: PERSONALIZING THE MESSAGE

1. What kinds of situations most tempt you to feel anxious or out of control?

2. In what ways does modern culture encourage people to rely on themselves rather than trust God?

3. What area of your life feels most difficult to surrender fully to God's authority?

4. Have you ever experienced a season where God seemed silent, but later you realized He was working behind the scenes?

SECTION 2: SCRIPTURE DISCOVERY

KEY POINT 1: The Kingdom of God Invites Us to Trust God's Reign

Scriptures: Mark 1:15; Matthew 6:25–33; Luke 17:20–21

Scripture Insights:

Jesus announced that the Kingdom of God had arrived through His presence and ministry. The Kingdom is not merely future—it is God's active reign breaking into present life. Jesus teaches that anxiety decreases when trust in God's authority increases. Seeking God's Kingdom first means allowing His rule to become the governing reality of our lives rather than fear, control, or uncertainty.

Discussion Questions:

1. Read Mark 1:15. What was Jesus calling people to do in response to the arrival of God's Kingdom?

2. According to Matthew 6:25–32, what kinds of worries does Jesus address?

3. Why does worry often reveal deeper struggles with trust and control?

4. Read Matthew 6:33. What changes when God's Kingdom becomes our highest priority?

5. What area of your life needs to come more fully under God's reign right now?

KEY POINT 2: God's Kingdom Is Revealed to Hearts Willing to Receive It

Scriptures: Mark 4:11; Matthew 13:11; Luke 17:20–21

Scripture Insights:

Jesus described the Kingdom as a "secret" not because God wants to hide truth, but because spiritual realities must be received through revelation and surrender. The Kingdom cannot be fully understood through observation or human reasoning alone. Hearts that are humble, receptive, and willing to submit to God's authority are able to recognize and participate in His Kingdom.

Discussion Questions:

1. Read Mark 4:11. Why did Jesus describe the Kingdom as a "secret"?

2. How can someone hear Jesus' teachings yet still miss the reality of God's Kingdom?

3. Why is spiritual surrender necessary for understanding spiritual truth?

4. What does it mean to live under God's authority rather than merely know about it intellectually?

5. How can believers cultivate hearts that are receptive to God's Kingdom?

KEY POINT 3: God's Kingdom Reorders Our Values and Priorities

Scriptures: Colossians 3:1–3; Romans 14:17; Psalm 110:1

Scripture Insights:

When God's Kingdom takes root in a person's life, priorities begin to shift. Identity is no longer anchored in success, comparison, achievement, or control, but in Christ's reign and security. Kingdom living produces righteousness, peace, and joy through the Holy Spirit. As believers align their hearts with Christ's authority, life becomes more centered, stable, and spiritually grounded.

Discussion Questions:

1. Read Colossians 3:1–3. What does Paul mean by setting our minds on "things above"?

2. How does knowing your life is "hidden with Christ" affect fear and insecurity?

3. According to Romans 14:17, what truly defines the Kingdom of God?

4. Why do misplaced priorities often create inner conflict and anxiety?

5. What practical changes might happen when Christ's reign becomes central in daily life?

KEY POINT 4: God's Kingdom Often Grows Quietly and Gradually

Scriptures: Matthew 13:31–32; Galatians 6:9

Scripture Insights:

Jesus taught that God's Kingdom often begins in small, hidden, and seemingly insignificant ways—like a mustard seed planted in the ground. God frequently works beneath the surface before visible results appear. Spiritual growth, transformation, and divine purpose often unfold gradually through faithful obedience, patience, and trust in God's ti ming.

Discussion Questions:

1. Read Matthew 13:31–32. Why did Jesus compare the Kingdom to a mustard seed?

2. What does this parable teach about small beginnings and gradual growth?

3. Why do people sometimes become discouraged during seasons when progress feels slow?

4. Read Galatians 6:9. What encouragement does Paul give believers who feel weary?

5. What area of your life currently requires patience and trust in God's process?

KEY POINT 5: Under God's Kingdom, God Is Always at Work

Behind the Scenes

Scriptures: Genesis 45:5–8; Genesis 50:20; Ruth 2:3; Romans 8:28–29

Scripture Insights:

The stories of Joseph and Ruth reveal that God is actively working even during painful, uncertain, or hidden seasons. What appears random, delayed, or confusing from a human perspective is often part of God's larger redemptive plan. Under God's Kingdom, delay is not denial and waiting is never wasted. God faithfully works through suffering, ordinary obedience, and hidden seasons to accomplish His purposes.

Discussion Questions:

1. Read Genesis 50:20. How did Joseph reinterpret his suffering later in life?

2. Why is it often difficult to recognize God's activity during painful seasons?

3. Read Ruth 2:3. What appears accidental in Ruth's story that later proves providential?

4. How does Romans 8:28–29 encourage believers during seasons of uncertainty?

5. What current situation in your life requires greater trust that God is working behind the scenes?

F. SECTION 3: PERSONAL APPLICATION & REFLECTION

1. In what area of your life do you most need to trust God's reign instead of giving in to anxiety?

2. What priorities may need to be reordered under Christ's authority?

3. Are you currently in a season of waiting, hiddenness, or uncertainty? How is God shaping you through it?

4. What practical step can you take this week to live more intentionally under God's Kingdom?

G. CLOSING WISDOM KEYS

1. God's Kingdom invites us to trust His reign instead of living controlled by fear and anxiety.

2. When Christ's rule becomes central, our priorities are reshaped around righteousness, peace, and joy through the Holy Spirit.

3. Under God's Kingdom, God is always working behind the scenes—even when His activity is not immediately visible.

H. PRAYER

I. PRAYER POINTS

1. Ask God to help you trust His reign more deeply in every area of life.

2. Pray for Kingdom priorities to shape your decisions, relationships, and daily habits.

3. Present your personal burdens, anxieties, and uncertainties before God.

4. Ask the Holy Spirit to strengthen your faith during seasons of waiting, hiddenness, or discouragement.

Ask for individual prayer requests and pray for the individual needs of your group members and any area the Spirit directs.

II. CLOSING PRAYER

Heavenly Father, thank You for revealing the reality of Your Kingdom through Jesus Christ. Help us trust Your reign even when life feels uncertain or chaotic. Teach us to seek Your Kingdom first and to align our priorities with Your will. Strengthen us during seasons when Your work seems hidden, and remind us that You are always faithful and always at work. Let righteousness, peace, and joy through the Holy Spirit shape our lives daily as we live under Your rule. In Jesus' name, Amen.

Use the Chapter 2 Believer Declarations during the week.

KEY TRUTH TO REMEMBER

Under God's Kingdom, trust replaces anxiety, priorities are reshaped, and God is always at work—even when we cannot see it.

DAILY BELIEVER DECLARATIONS (CHAPTER 2)

The Secret of the Kingdom of God

Day 1 — Trusting God's Reign Over Anxiety

Scripture: Matthew 6:25–33

Declaration: Under God's Kingdom, I choose trust over anxiety. God reigns over my life, my needs, and my future. I release control and rest in my Father's care.

Prayer: Father, I surrender my worries to You today. Help me trust Your reign over every concern. In Jesus' name. In Jesus' name. Amen.

Day 2 — Living Under God's Kingdom Rule

Scripture: Luke 17:20–21

Declaration: God's Kingdom is present and active in my life. As I submit my heart to His reign, His rule shapes my daily choices.

Prayer: Lord Jesus, let Your Kingdom rule my heart and guide my steps today. In Your name Amen.

Day 3 — Kingdom Priorities: Righteousness, Peace, and Joy

Scripture: Romans 14:17

Declaration: God's Kingdom shapes my life from the inside out. Righteousness anchors me, peace guards me, and joy sustains me through the Holy Spirit.

Prayer: Holy Spirit, fill my heart with Kingdom righteousness, peace, and joy today. In Jesus' name. In Jesus' name. Amen.

Day 4 — Setting My Mind on Things Above

Scripture: Colossians 3:1–3

Declaration: My life is hidden with Christ in God. I set my heart and mind on Christ's reign, not earthly pressure or fear.

Prayer: Jesus, help me live from my secure identity in You and align my priorities with Your Kingdom. In Your name. Amen.

Day 5 — Trusting God's Hidden Work

Scripture: Matthew 13:31–32

Declaration: Under God's Kingdom, small beginnings matter. Even when I cannot see it, God is growing something good in my life.

Prayer: Lord Jesus, give me faith to trust Your work in hidden and quiet seasons. In Your name Amen.

Day 6 — Waiting Without Giving Up

Scripture: Galatians 6:9

Declaration: I will not grow weary in doing good. Under God's Kingdom, waiting is not wasted, and faithfulness will bear fruit in due time.

Prayer: Father, strengthen me to remain faithful and patient as I wait on You. In Jesus' name. In Jesus' name. Amen.

Day 7 — God Is Working All Things for Good

Scripture: Romans 8:28–29

Declaration: God is always at work in my life under His Kingdom.

Even in unseen seasons, He is forming me and fulfilling His good purposes.

Prayer: Thank You, Lord Jesus, for working behind the scenes of my life. I trust Your process and Your timing. In Your name Amen.

Chapter 3 Study Guide: The Secret of Deliverance from the Kingdom of Darkness

A. SESSION AIM

To help participants understand that God's Kingdom operates with real authority, that Christ has already defeated darkness through the cross, and that believers now live from His finished victory through faith-filled obedience rather than fear or striving.

B. ICE BREAKER

What is an example of authority you respect because it is exercised calmly, confidently, and consistently rather than forcefully?

Leader Note: Encourage practical examples from daily life. Help participants begin thinking about authority that flows from position, character, and alignment rather than intimidation or control.

C. OPEN YOUR SESSION WITH PRAYER

Invite someone to open in prayer, or use the prayer below:

Heavenly Father, thank You for the victory You have given us through Jesus Christ. Open our hearts today to understand the authority of Your Kingdom and the freedom we now have in Christ. Strengthen our faith, remove fear and discouragement, and help us live confidently under Your reign. Let Your truth renew our minds and shape how we respond to opposition, temptation, and struggle. In Jesus' name, Amen.

D. INTRODUCTION (CHAPTER 3 SUMMARY)

Many believers sincerely love God yet still feel intimidated by fear, recurring struggles, spiritual opposition, or uncertainty. Scripture explains that this tension exists because the Kingdom of God is not passive—it confronts everything that opposes God's rule. Wherever God's Kingdom advances, darkness resists.

But the good news of the gospel is that Jesus Christ has already secured victory. Through His life, death, and resurrection, He defeated the power of sin, broke the authority of darkness, and established His Kingdom in power. Believers are no longer living under the dominion of darkness but have been transferred into the Kingdom of God's beloved S on.

This chapter reveals that Kingdom authority is not about human striving, emotional intensity, or religious performance. It flows from surrender to Christ's reign. As believers live in faith-filled obedience, the authority and victory of Christ become visible in everyday life.

E. BIBLE DISCUSSION

SECTION 1: PERSONALIZING THE MESSAGE

1. When do you most feel spiritually discouraged, intimidated, or powerless?

2. Why do you think many believers struggle to live confidently in Christ's authority?

3. Have you ever experienced a situation where God gave you peace or strength in themiddle of spiritual or emotional opposition?

4. What does it personally mean to you that Christ has already won the victory over darkness?

SECTION 2: SCRIPTURE DISCOVERY

KEY POINT 1: The Kingdom of God Operates with Authority and Power

Scriptures: 1 Corinthians 4:20; Mark 9:1; Matthew 10:1, 7–8

Scripture Insights: The Kingdom of God is not merely a message to discuss intellectually—it is the active reign of God demonstrated through authority and power. Jesus did not only teach truth; He confronted darkness, healed the broken, and demonstrated God's rule in action. Kingdom authority flows from alignment with God's reign rather than human effort or performance.

Discussion Questions:

1. Read 1 Corinthians 4:20. What does Paul mean when he says the Kingdom is "not a matter of talk but of power"?

2. Why can religious activity exist without true spiritual authority?

3. According to Matthew 10:1, 7–8, what authority did Jesus give His disciples?

4. hy does submission to God matter in living with spiritual authority?

5. What areas of your life need greater alignment under Christ's authority?

KEY POINT 2: Jesus Came to Confront and Defeat Darkness

Scriptures: 1 John 3:8; John 12:46; Acts 26:18

Scripture Insights: Jesus came not merely to improve lives externally but to destroy the works of darkness and bring people into God's Kingdom. Through Christ, people are transferred from darkness into light and from Satan's power into God's reign. Every act of healing, deliverance, forgiveness, and restoration in Jesus' ministry demonstrated that God's Kingdom was advancing against the powers of darkness.

Discussion Questions:

1. Read 1 John 3:8. According to this verse, why did Jesus appear?

2. How does Jesus describe His mission in John 12:46?

3. Why does darkness often resist the truth and light of Christ?

4. Read Acts 26:18. What changes occur when someone is brought into God's Kingdom?

5. How does understanding Christ's mission strengthen believers facing fear or spiritual opposition?

KEY POINT 3: Christ's Victory Was Accomplished Through the Cross

Scriptures: Colossians 1:13–14; Colossians 2:13–15; Revelation 12:10–11

Scripture Insights: The cross of Christ was not defeat—it was God's decisive triumph over sin, accusation, and the powers of darkness. Through Jesus' death and resurrection, believers were rescued from the dominion of darkness and transferred into Christ's Kingdom. Satan's authority to accuse has been broken because the debt of sin has been fully canceled through the blood of Christ.

Discussion Questions:

1. Read Colossians 1:13–14. What does Paul mean by being "rescued from the dominion of darkness"?

2. According to Colossians 2:13–15, what did God accomplish through the cross?

3. Why is it important to understand that believers fight from victory rather than for victory?

4. Read Revelation 12:10–11. How do believers overcome the accuser?

5. How does Christ's finished victory change the way believers face fear, guilt, or condemnation?

KEY POINT 4: Kingdom Authority Is Realized Through Submission and Obedience

Scriptures: James 4:7; Mark 1:15; Matthew 7:21–23

Scripture Insights: Kingdom authority is not self-generated—it flows from surrender to God's reign. Scripture teaches that believers cannot effectively resist darkness while resisting God. Obedience, repentance, and submission position believers under Christ's authority. The Kingdom is not merely admired intellectually; it is experienced through lives aligned with God's will.

Discussion Questions:

1. Read James 4:7. Why does James place submission before resistance?

2. What does genuine repentance involve according to Jesus' Kingdom teaching?

3. Why is outward religious activity alone insufficient according to Matthew 7:21–23?

4. How does obedience reveal genuine trust in God?

5. What practical area of your life may require deeper surrender to Christ's authority?

KEY POINT 5: God's Kingdom Is Revealed Through Faith-Filled Obedience

Scriptures: James 2:17–18; Romans 1:5; Luke 11:20

Scripture Insights: The authority of God's Kingdom becomes visible through everyday faithfulness and obedience. Faith in Scripture is never passive—it responds, trusts, and acts. God works through surrendered lives in ordinary moments, quiet decisions, and faithful obedience. Kingdom power is not reserved only for dramatic moments but is revealed through believers who consistently trust and obey God.

Discussion Questions:

1. Read James 2:17–18. What relationship does James describe between faith and action?

2. Why does obedience matter in experiencing God's Kingdom?

3. According to Romans 1:5, how are belief and obedience connected?

4. Read Luke 11:20. What did Jesus say demonstrated the arrival of God's Kingdom?

5. What simple act of obedience might God be calling you to take this week?

F. SECTION 3: PERSONAL APPLICATION & REFLECTION

1. In what area of life do you most need to rely on Christ's authority instead of your own strength?

2. Are there fears, lies, or old patterns that you need to stop allowing to define your identity?

3. What does living from Christ's finished victory practically look like in your daily life?

4. What step of faith-filled obedience is God inviting you to take this week?

G. CLOSING WISDOM KEYS

1. God's Kingdom operates with real authority and power, not empty religious words.

2. Through the cross, Christ has already defeated darkness and secured victory for believers.

3. Kingdom authority becomes visible as believers live in surrender, faith, and obedience to Christ.

H. PRAYER

I. PRAYER POINTS

1. Ask God to help you live confidently under Christ's authority rather than fear or discouragement.

2. Pray for freedom from spiritual intimidation, condemnation, and lingering fear.

3. Present your personal struggles, temptations, or battles before God and ask for strength and wisdom.

4. Ask the Holy Spirit to help you walk daily in faith-filled obedience and confidence in Christ's finished victory.

Ask for individual prayer requests and pray for the individual needs of your group members and any area the Spirit directs.

II. CLOSING PRAYER

Heavenly Father, thank You for rescuing us from the dominion of darkness and bringing us into the Kingdom of Your Son. Thank You that Christ has already defeated sin, accusation, and the powers of darkness through the cross. Help us live confidently under Your authority and not be ruled by fear, discouragement, or striving. Teach us to trust You, obey Your Word, and walk daily in the victory Jesus has already secured. Let Your Kingdom become visible through our lives as we follow You in faith and obedience. In Jesus' name, Amen.

Use the Chapter 3 Daily Believer Declarations during the week.

KEY TRUTH TO REMEMBER

Under God's Kingdom, Christ reigns with authority, darkness has been defeated, and we live from His finished victory—not fear.

DAILY BELIEVER DECLARATIONS (CHAPTER 3)

The Secret of Deliverance from the Kingdom of Darkness

Day 1 — Living Under Kingdom Authority

Scripture: 1 Corinthians 4:20

Declaration: Under God's Kingdom, I live from Christ's authority, not my own strength. God's power is at work in my life as I submit to His reign.

Prayer: Father, help me live today under Your authority. Teach me to rely on Your power rather than my own efforts. In Jesus' name. Amen.

Day 2 — Standing in Christ's Victory

Scripture: Colossians 2:13–15

Declaration: Christ's victory defines my reality, not darkness or fear. I stand in what Jesus has already accomplished for me.

Prayer: Lord Jesus, thank You for Your finished work on the cross. Help me live today with confidence in Your victory. In Your name. Amen.

Day 3 — Freedom from Darkness

Scripture: Acts 26:18

Declaration: I have been transferred from darkness to light and from Satan's power to God. I walk in freedom, forgiveness, and hope under God's Kingdom.

Prayer: God, thank You for delivering me from darkness. Open my eyes to walk fully in the freedom You have given me. In Jesus' name. Amen.

Day 4 — The Purpose of Christ's Coming

Scripture: 1 John 3:8

Declaration: Jesus came to destroy the works of the devil. Under God's Kingdom, darkness has no authority over my life.

Prayer: Lord, remind me today that You have overcome sin and darkness. Help me live boldly in the freedom You provide. In Your name. Amen.

Day 5 — Obedience as Faith in Action

Scripture: James 2:17

Declaration: My faith is alive and active through obedience. As I trust God and act on His Word, His Kingdom is realized through my life.

Prayer: Father, strengthen my faith to act in obedience today. Let my life reflect trust in You, not just words. In Jesus' name. Amen.

Day 6 — Alignment Under God's Reign

Scripture: James 4:7

Declaration: As I submit myself to God, I stand under His authority. The enemy has no power where God's reign is honored.

Prayer: Lord, I surrender every area of my life to You today. Help me resist what opposes You by remaining aligned with Your will. In Jesus' name. Amen.

Day 7 — Kingdom Power in Everyday Life

Scripture: Luke 11:20

Declaration: God's Kingdom is present and active in my life. Through faith-filled obedience, God's power is at work through me.

Prayer: Holy Spirit, work through my obedience today. Let Your Kingdom be seen in my actions, attitudes, and choices. In Jesus' name. A men.

KEY TRUTH TO REMEMBER

Under God's Kingdom, we live under Christ's authority, stand in His victory, and walk in obedient faith—confident that God's power is at work through us.

CHAPTER 4 STUDY GUIDE: THE SECRET OF CHRIST IN YOU

A. SESSION AIM

To help participants move from striving to abiding by understanding that the Christian life flows from Christ living within us, not from self-effort or spiritual performance.

B. ICE BREAKER

What is something in life that only functions properly when it remains connected to its source—and what happens when that connection is lost?

Leader Note: Encourage practical examples from daily life. Help participants begin thinking about dependence, connection, and the importance of remaining connected to the true source of life and power.

C. OPEN YOUR SESSION WITH PRAYER

Invite someone to open in prayer, or use the prayer below:

Heavenly Father, thank You for the gift of Your presence within us through Christ. Open our hearts today to understand what it means to live from Christ rather than striving in our own strength. Teach us how to abide in You more deeply and help us rest in the life You already provide. Let this discussion bring freedom, renewal, and greater dependence on You. In Jesus' name, Amen.

D. INTRODUCTION (CHAPTER 4 SUMMARY)

Many sincere believers quietly carry spiritual exhaustion. They love God, desire to grow, and want to live faithfully—yet over time the Christian life can begin to feel heavy, pressured, and unsustainable. Instead of experiencing peace, believers often feel trapped in cycles of striving, comparison, self-effort, and discouragement.

But the gospel reveals a radically different reality. Christianity is not primarily about trying harder to live for Christ—it is about learning to live from Christ who already lives within us. Scripture calls this truth a mystery once hidden but now revealed: "Christ in you, the hope of glory."

This changes everything. The Christian life was never meant to be sustained by willpower alone. God has not simply forgiven believers and then left them to manage spiritual growth independently. Through the indwelling presence of Christ, God Himself becomes the source of strength, obedience, endurance, and transformation. Spiritual fruit grows not through striving, but through abiding in Christ.

In this session, we will explore how Christ within us becomes the source of spiritual life, how freedom from striving comes through dependence, and how abiding in Christ naturally produces lasting fruit.

E. BIBLE DISCUSSION

SECTION 1: PERSONALIZING THE MESSAGE

1. Have you ever experienced a season where your faith felt more exhausting than life-giving?

2. What are some ways believers unintentionally fall into striving or performance-based Christianity?

3. When do you most tend to rely on your own strength rather than depend on Christ?

4. What would change if you truly believed Christ's life was already present within you?

SECTION 2: SCRIPTURE DISCOVERY

KEY POINT 1: Christ in You Is the Source of the Christian Life

Scriptures: Colossians 1:26–27; Romans 8:10; Ephesians 3:16–17

Scripture Insights: The heart of the Christian life is not self-improvement but Christ's indwelling presence. Scripture reveals the mystery of "Christ in you" as the true source of spiritual life, hope, and transformation. Believers are not expected to generate spiritual strength independently; Christ Himself lives within them through the Holy Spirit and becomes the source of life from the inside out.

Discussion Questions:

1. Read Colossians 1:26–27. What does Paul describe as the great mystery now revealed?

2. Why is "Christ in you" different from merely trying to imitate Christ externally?

3. According to Romans 8:10, what gives believers spiritual life even in human weakness?

4. Why do many believers still try to live the Christian life through self-effort?

5. What area of your life most needs deeper dependence on Christ as your source?

KEY POINT 2: Freedom from Striving Comes Through Christ's Life Within Us

Scriptures: Galatians 2:20; 2 Corinthians 5:14–15

Scripture Insights: Paul teaches that the Christian life is no longer powered by self-reliance but by Christ living within believers. "Not I, but Christ" represents freedom from carrying spiritual life through human effort. Obedience flows not from pressure, fear, or performance, but from Christ's love taking hold of the believer's heart and producing trust-filled dependence.

Discussion Questions:

1. Read Galatians 2:20. What does Paul mean when he says, "I no longer live, but Christ lives in me"?

2. How does this verse challenge performance-based or pressure-driven Christianity?

3. According to 2 Corinthians 5:14–15, what now motivates Paul's life?

4. Why does striving eventually lead to exhaustion and discouragement?

5. What practical difference exists between trying harder and depending more deeply on Christ?

KEY POINT 3: Spiritual Growth Happens Through Abiding, Not Striving

Scriptures: John 15:4–5; John 15:7

Scripture Insights:

Jesus teaches that spiritual fruitfulness comes through remaining connected to Him like branches connected to a vine. A branch does not produce fruit through effort but through connection to the source of life. In the same way, believers bear spiritual fruit as they abide in Christ through ongoing trust, surrender, prayer, and dependence.

Discussion Questions:

1. Read John 15:4–5. Why does Jesus compare believers to branches connected to a vine?

2. What happens spiritually when believers try to function independently from Christ?

3. Why does Jesus emphasize remaining or abiding rather than striving?

4. According to John 15:7, how does abiding affect prayer?

5. What habits or practices help believers remain connected to Christ daily?

KEY POINT 4: Prayer Flows from Relationship Rather Than Obligation

Scriptures: John 15:7; Ephesians 6:18

Scripture Insights:

As believers abide in Christ, their desires and prayers begin to align with God's heart and purposes. Prayer becomes less about religious obligation or trying to persuade God and more about participating in the life and will of God through ongoing relationship. Spirit-led prayer flows naturally from abiding communion with Christ.

Discussion Questions:

1. Read John 15:7. What conditions does Jesus connect to effective prayer?

2. How does abiding in Christ reshape what believers desire and ask for?

3. Why is prayer often difficult when it becomes disconnected from relationship?

4. According to Ephesians 6:18, what does it mean to pray in the Spirit?

5. How can prayer become more relational and less routine in your

daily life?

KEY POINT 5: Christ's Life Produces Lasting Fruit Through Ordinary Faithfulness

Scriptures: John 15:5; Colossians 1:27; Galatians 5:22–23

Scripture Insights:

God never intended believers to manufacture spiritual fruit through pressure or performance. As Christ's life flows through believers, the Holy Spirit gradually produces Christlike character, endurance, love, and faithfulness. Spiritual growth often happens quietly and progressively as believers remain connected to Christ in everyday life.

Discussion Questions:

1. Read Galatians 5:22–23. Why is spiritual fruit described as the "fruit of the Spirit"?

2. Why does genuine fruit take time to grow?

3. How does abiding produce sustainable spiritual growth?

4. What kinds of "artificial fruit" do believers sometimes try to display outwardly?

5. What evidence of Christ's life growing in you have you noticed recently?

F. SECTION 3: PERSONAL APPLICATION & REFLECTION

1. Where in your life are you most tempted to strive instead of abide?

2. What would it look like practically to live more consciously from "Christ in you"?

3. How can you shift your spiritual habits from pressure-driven to relationship-driven?

4. What step can you take this week to remain more intentionally connected to Christ?

G. CLOSING WISDOM KEYS

1. The Christian life is sustained by Christ's indwelling presence, not by human striving.

2. Freedom from exhaustion comes when believers learn to live from Christ rather than merely for Christ.

3. Spiritual fruit grows naturally as believers remain connected to Christ through abiding relationship.

H. PRAYER

I. PRAYER POINTS

1. Ask God to help you rely more deeply on Christ's life within you instead of your own strength.

2. Pray for freedom from striving, comparison, pressure, and performance-based faith.

3. Present your personal burdens, weaknesses, and areas of exhaustion before God.

4. Ask the Holy Spirit to deepen your awareness of Christ's presence and teach you to abide daily in Him.

Ask for individual prayer requests and pray for the individual needs of your group members and any area the Spirit directs.

II. CLOSING PRAYER

Heavenly Father, thank You that the Christian life is not something we must carry alone. Thank You for the gift of Christ living within us. Teach us to stop striving in our own strength and to live from the life You have already placed within us. Help us remain connected to You through prayer, trust, surrender, and obedience. Produce lasting fruit in our lives through the power of Your Spirit. Strengthen weary hearts, restore joy,

and help us rest confidently in Christ's sufficiency. In Jesus' name, Amen
.

Use the Chapter 4 Daily Believer Declarations during the week.

KEY TRUTH TO REMEMBER

The Christian life is not lived by effort for Christ, but by Christ living His life through us.

The Secret of Christ in You

Day 1 — Christ Lives in Me

Scripture: Colossians 1:27

Declaration: Christ lives in me — the hope of glory.

Wisdom Key: The Christian life is not lived alone; it is Christ's life expressed through me.

Prayer: Lord Jesus, thank You for dwelling within me. Help me remember that I am never alone and never without Your strength. In Your name, Amen.

Day 2 — I Live from His Strength

Scripture: Galatians 2:20

Declaration: The life I now live, I live by faith in the Son of God.

Wisdom Key: Christ does not call me to live for Him in my own strength, but to live through Him by faith.

Prayer: Father, teach me to depend on Christ's life within me rather than striving in my own effort. In Jesus' name. Amen.

Day 3 — I Am Empowered by Resurrection Life

Scripture: Romans 8:11

Declaration: The Spirit who raised Jesus from the dead lives in me.

Wisdom Key: Resurrection power is not only future hope — it is present reality.

Prayer: Holy Spirit, empower my obedience and renew my heart today. In Jesus' name. Amen.

Day 4 — My Identity Is Anchored in Christ

Scripture: 2 Corinthians 5:17

Declaration: I am a new creation in Christ.

Wisdom Key: My identity is defined by union with Christ, not by my past.

Prayer: Lord Jesus, free me from shame and remind me that I belong to You. Shape my thinking according to who I am in Christ. In Your name, A men.

Day 5 — I Abide, I Do Not Strive

Scripture: John 15:4–5

Declaration: As I remain in Christ, I bear fruit.

Wisdom Key: Fruit grows from abiding, not from pressure.

Prayer: Jesus, teach me to abide in You daily. Let Your life flow through mine. In Your name, Amen.

Day 6 — Christ Is My Source, Not My Performance

Scripture: Philippians 2:13

Declaration: God works in me to will and to act according to His good purpose.

Wisdom Key: Transformation is Spirit-driven, not self-manufactured.

Prayer: Father, help me cooperate with Your grace and rest in Your work within me. In Jesus' name. Amen.

Day 7 — I Walk in Hope Because He Is Within Me

Scripture: John 14:23

Declaration: Christ dwells with me and in me.

Wisdom Key: The indwelling presence of Christ is my daily assurance.

Prayer: Lord Jesus, let Your presence shape my thoughts, my choices, and my confidence today. In Your name, Amen.

Chapter 5 Study Guide: Living as a Kingdom Representative in a Broken World

A. SESSION AIM

To help participants understand that Christian mission flows from identity and union with Christ rather than pressure or performance, and that God uses ordinary faithfulness to make His Kingdom visible in the world.

B. ICE BREAKER

What is something that makes a difference simply by being present rather than by trying harder?

Leader Note: Encourage participants to think about everyday examples. Help the group begin considering how presence itself can carry influence and impact without force or striving.

C. OPEN YOUR SESSION WITH PRAYER

Invite someone to open in prayer, or use the prayer below:

Heavenly Father, thank You for allowing us to participate in Your Kingdom work. Help us understand that we do not carry the mission alone, but that Christ is already at work within us. Teach us to live faithfully and represent You well in our everyday lives. Open our hearts to Your Spirit and help us see opportunities to reflect Your love, truth, and grace in the world around us. In Jesus' name, Amen.

D. INTRODUCTION (CHAPTER 5 SUMMARY)

Many believers quietly wonder whether their ordinary lives truly matter in God's larger plan. Some feel pressure to do more for God, while others feel inadequate, uncertain, or unequipped to make a meaningful impact. Yet Scripture reveals something deeply freeing: God's Kingdom is often made visible not through extraordinary performance, but through ordinary faithfulness shaped by Christ's presence within us.

Jesus never told His followers to manufacture light—He declared that they already are light because His life now lives within them. The mission of God is not something believers carry independently; it is participation in what God is already doing through Christ and the Holy Spirit. God works through everyday conversations, ordinary acts of obedience, quiet integrity, and faithful presence in daily life.

This chapter reminds us that Christian witness flows from identity, not pressure; from presence, not performance; and from Christ's life within us, not our own striving. As believers live openly from union with Christ, God uses ordinary lives to accomplish extraordinary Kingdom purposes.

E. BIBLE DISCUSSION

SECTION 1: PERSONALIZING THE MESSAGE

1. Have you ever felt pressure to "perform" spiritually or feel useful to God?

2. Why do many believers underestimate the importance of everyday faithfulness?

3. What ordinary places or relationships make up most of your daily life right now?

4. How does it change your perspective to realize God may already be working through you in unseen ways?

SECTION 2: SCRIPTURE DISCOVERY

KEY POINT 1: You Are Already Light in Christ

Scriptures: Matthew 5:14–16; John 8:12; Ephesians 5:8

Scripture Insights: Jesus does not tell believers to become light—He declares that they already are light because His life is now within them. Christian witness flows from identity rather than pressure or performance. As believers walk in humble obedience and dependence on Christ, His light naturally becomes visible through their lives, attitudes, and actions.

Discussion Questions:

1. Read Matthew 5:14–16. What does Jesus say His followers already are?

2. Why is it important that Jesus begins with identity rather than command?

3. According to John 8:12, where does the believer's light originate?

4. What does it practically mean to "live as children of light" according to Ephesians 5:8?

5. How can believers allow Christ's light to be visible naturally rather than forcefully?

KEY POINT 2: God Is Already Reconciling the World to Himself

Scriptures: 2 Corinthians 5:17–20; John 20:21; John 4:38

Scripture Insights: God's work of reconciliation began through Christ long before believers participate in it. Christians are not responsible for carrying the mission alone or producing spiritual results through pressure and striving. Instead, believers are ambassadors who faithfully represent the reconciliation God has already accomplished through Jesus Christ.

Discussion Questions:

1. Read 2 Corinthians 5:17–20. What does Paul say God is already doing in the world?

2. How does being an ambassador differ from being responsible for results?

3. Why is reconciliation ultimately God's work rather than ours?

4. According to John 20:21, how does Jesus send His followers?

5. How does understanding that God is already at work remove pressure from Christian witness?

KEY POINT 3: God Uses Ordinary Lives for Extraordinary Kingdom Purposes

Scriptures: Acts 8:4; 1 Corinthians 1:26–27; Luke 16:10

Scripture Insights: Throughout Scripture, God advances His Kingdom through ordinary believers living faithful lives. The spread of the gospel in the early church often happened through scattered, unnamed believers simply living faithfully wherever they went. God's power is revealed not through human impressiveness but through humble dependence and consistent obedience.

Discussion Questions:

1. Read Acts 8:4. Who was spreading the gospel in this passage?

2. Why does God often choose ordinary people to accomplish His purposes?

3. According to Luke 16:10, why does faithfulness in small things matter?

4. How does God's use of ordinary believers encourage you personally?

5. What "ordinary" part of your life may actually carry Kingdom

significance?

KEY POINT 4: Kingdom Representation Happens Through Everyday Faithfulness

Scriptures: Galatians 6:9; 2 Corinthians 3:5; Colossians 1:27

Scripture Insights: God honors quiet faithfulness even when its impact is not immediately visible. The Christian life is not about chasing visibility or success but about faithfully living from Christ's presence within us. As believers remain faithful in ordinary conversations, decisions, relationships, and responsibilities, God works through those moments to reveal His Kingdom.

Discussion Questions:

1. Read Galatians 6:9. Why does Paul encourage believers not to grow weary?

2. According to 2 Corinthians 3:5, where does spiritual sufficiency come from?

3. Why is unseen faithfulness often difficult to value?

4. How does "Christ in you" give meaning to ordinary daily life?

5. What small act of faithfulness might God be calling you to continue even if you cannot yet see results?

KEY POINT 5: Faithfulness, Not Visibility, Defines Success in God's Kingdom

Scriptures: Luke 16:10; 1 Corinthians 15:9–10; Matthew 5:16

Scripture Insights: God measures success differently than the world does. Kingdom impact is not primarily about recognition, visibility, or outward impressiveness. God values humble faithfulness, surrendered lives, and quiet obedience. As believers simply live from Christ's life within them, God brings fruit and influence according to His purposes and timing.

Discussion Questions:

1. Why do people often associate significance with visibility or public recognition?

2. How does Paul's humility in 1 Corinthians 15:9–10 reshape our understanding of usefulness to God?

3. What does Matthew 5:16 teach about the purpose of good works?

4. How can believers remain faithful without becoming discouraged by lack of visible results?

5. What would it look like for you to measure success by faithfulness rather than recognition?

F. SECTION 3: PERSONAL APPLICATION & REFLECTION

1. Where might God be inviting you to live more openly from your identity in Christ?

2. What ordinary relationship or environment may be a place for Kingdom influence right now?

3. Are there areas where pressure or comparison have replaced simple faithfulness?

4. What practical step can you take this week to represent Christ more intentionally in everyday life?

G. CLOSING WISDOM KEYS

- Kingdom representation flows from identity in Christ, not pressure to perform.

- God is already reconciling the world to Himself, and believers are invited to participate in His work.

- Ordinary faithfulness becomes extraordinary when surrendered to Christ's Kingdom purposes.

H. PRAYER

I. PRAYER POINTS

1. Ask God to help you live confidently from your identity in Christ rather than pressure or comparison.

2. Pray for faithfulness, integrity, and sensitivity to the Holy Spirit in everyday life.

3. Present your relationships, workplace, responsibilities, and daily environments before God.

4. Ask the Holy Spirit to help Christ's light shine naturally through your life and actions.

Ask for individual prayer requests and pray for the individual needs of your group members and any area the Spirit directs.

II. CLOSING PRAYER

Heavenly Father, thank You for allowing us to participate in Your Kingdom work through everyday faithfulness. Thank You that we do not carry the mission alone, but that Christ lives within us and works through us. Help us stop striving for recognition or performance and instead live faithfully from our identity in Christ. Use our conversations, attitudes, decisions, and ordinary moments to reveal Your love and truth to others. Strengthen us to remain faithful, trusting that You are working even when we cannot immediately see the results. In Jesus' name, Amen.

Use the Chapter 5 Daily Believer Declarations during the week.

KEY TRUTH TO REMEMBER

We don't bring the Kingdom by trying harder—Christ in us makes the Kingdom visible through our everyday faithfulness.

Living as a Kingdom Representative in a Broken World

Day 1 — I Am Light

Scripture: Matthew 5:14

Declaration: I am the light of the world because Christ lives in me. I do not strive to shine; I live from His light within me.

Prayer: Lord Jesus, help me live today from who I already am in You. In Your name. In Your name, Amen.

Day 2 — Sent from Peace, Not Pressure

Scripture: John 20:21

Declaration: I am sent by Jesus from a place of peace and confidence. I carry forward what Christ has already accomplished.

Prayer: Father, help me walk today in the peace of Christ's finished work. In Jesus' name. In Jesus' name. Amen.

Day 3 — A Minister of Reconciliation

Scripture: 2 Corinthians 5:18–19

Declaration: God is reconciling the world to Himself, and I participate in His work. I am an ambassador of grace, not a producer of results.

Prayer: Holy Spirit, guide my words and actions as I represent Christ today. In Jesus' name. In Jesus' name. Amen.

Day 4 — God Uses the Ordinary

Scripture: 1 Corinthians 1:27

Declaration: God uses ordinary people like me to display His power. I trust God to work through my faithfulness.

Prayer: Lord Jesus, thank You for using ordinary lives to accomplish Your purposes. In Your name. Amen.

Day 5 — Faithful in Small Things

Scripture: Luke 16:10

Declaration: My faithfulness in small things matters deeply to God. I walk in obedience, trusting God with the results.

Prayer: God, help me remain faithful in the ordinary moments of today. In Jesus' name. Amen.

Day 6 — Do Not Grow Weary

Scripture: Galatians 6:9

Declaration: I will not grow weary in doing good. God is producing a harvest in His time.

Prayer: Father, strengthen me to remain faithful and patient as I walk with You. In Jesus' name. Amen.

Day 7 — Extraordinary Fruit from Ordinary Faithfulness

Scripture: John 15:16

Declaration: As I abide in Christ, my life bears lasting fruit. God brings extraordinary results through faithful obedience.

Prayer: Lord Jesus, help me trust You with the fruit You are producing through my life. In Your mighty name. Amen.

CHAPTER 6 STUDY GUIDE: THE SECRET OF SPIRITUAL WISDOM

A. SESSION AIM

To help participants understand that God's wisdom is revealed by the Spirit, received through trust and dependence, and walked out step by step as believers stay close to God and follow the Spirit's leading.

B. ICE BREAKER

What is something in life that requires patience, trust, and steady progress rather than quick answers or instant results?

Leader Note: Encourage practical examples. Help participants begin thinking about how growth, wisdom, and direction often unfold gradually over time rather than all at once.

C. OPEN YOUR SESSION WITH PRAYER

Invite someone to open in prayer, or use the prayer below:

Heavenly Father, thank You that You delight in giving wisdom to Your people. Open our hearts today to receive Your truth and help us depend more deeply on Your Spirit rather than our own understanding. Teach us to trust You when life feels uncertain and guide us step by step according to Your wisdom and timing. In Jesus' name, Amen.

D. INTRODUCTION (CHAPTER 6 SUMMARY)

One of the deepest struggles believers face is uncertainty about God's direction. Many sincerely desire to follow God yet still wrestle with confusion, difficult decisions, unanswered questions, and unclear paths. In those moments, believers often assume that wisdom belongs primarily to the highly intelligent, highly spiritual, or highly experienced.

But Scripture presents wisdom very differently. God's wisdom is not achieved through human effort or intellect alone—it is revealed by the Spirit to those who humbly depend on Him. Wisdom in Scripture is more than good decision-making; it is learning to see life from God's perspective and trust Him even when the full picture is not yet visible.

This chapter reminds us that God does not withhold wisdom to frustrate His people. He delights in revealing His wisdom as believers seek Him through prayer, Scripture, trust, attentiveness to the Spirit, and faithful obedience. God's guidance often unfolds slowly, steadily, and step by step—not because He is absent, but because He is forming trust and dependence within us.

In this session, we will explore how God reveals wisdom by the Spirit, how trust replaces self-reliance, and how the Holy Spirit faithfully guides believers in everyday life.

E. BIBLE DISCUSSION

SECTION 1: PERSONALIZING THE MESSAGE

1. What kinds of decisions or situations most make you feel uncertain or overwhelmed?

2. When life feels confusing, what are you most tempted to rely on besides God?

3. Have you ever experienced a time when God's guidance became clearer only after you trusted Him step by step?

4. What area of your life currently requires deeper trust in God's wisdom and timing?

SECTION 2: SCRIPTURE DISCOVERY

KEY POINT 1: God's Wisdom Is Revealed by the Spirit

Scriptures: 1 Corinthians 2:6–10; James 1:5

Scripture Insights: Scripture teaches that God's wisdom cannot be fully discovered through human intellect or reasoning alone. God's wisdom is revealed by the Holy Spirit to hearts that are humble, dependent, and willing to trust Him. Wisdom is not earned by ability but received through relationship with God and dependence on His Spirit.

Discussion Questions:

1. Read 1 Corinthians 2:6–10. How does Paul distinguish God's wisdom from human wisdom?

2. Why were even powerful and intelligent leaders unable to recognize God's wisdom fully?

3. According to James 1:5, what does God promise to those who ask for wisdom?

4. Why does asking God for wisdom require humility and dependence?

5. What area of your life currently needs God's wisdom most deeply?

KEY POINT 2: Trusting God's Wisdom Beyond Our Understanding

Scriptures: Proverbs 3:5–6; Exodus 23:29–30; Habakkuk 2:3

Scripture Insights: God's wisdom often requires believers to trust Him beyond what they can immediately understand or control. Scripture teaches that God directs lives step by step rather than revealing everything at once. His timing may feel slow, but His guidance is always wise, purposeful, and faithful. Trust grows as believers learn to lean on God's character rather than their own understanding.

Discussion Questions:

1. Read Proverbs 3:5–6. What does it practically mean to "lean not on your own understanding"?

2. Why is trusting God often difficult when clarity feels delayed?

3. According to Exodus 23:29–30, why did God choose to work "little by little"?

4. How does Habakkuk 2:3 encourage believers during seasons of waiting?

5. What situation in your life requires trusting God beyond your ability to fully understand?

KEY POINT 3: God's Wisdom Often Unfolds Step by Step

Scriptures: Habakkuk 2:3; Psalm 119:105; 1 Corinthians 2:10–12

Scripture Insights: God rarely reveals the entire journey all at once. Instead, He provides wisdom and direction step by step as believers continue walking with Him in trust. Like headlights illuminating only part of the road ahead, God's wisdom gives enough light for the next faithful step. As believers continue walking with the Spirit, greater clarity unfolds over time.

Discussion Questions:

1. Why do people often want complete clarity before taking action?

2. According to Psalm 119:105, how does God's Word guide believers?

3. How does 1 Corinthians 2:10–12 describe the Spirit's role in understanding God's wisdom?

4. Why might God intentionally reveal guidance gradually rather than instantly?

5. How can believers remain faithful during seasons when only the "next step" is clear?

KEY POINT 4: Walking in Wisdom Means Staying in Step with the Spirit

Scriptures: Galatians 5:25; John 14:26; John 16:13

Scripture Insights: The Holy Spirit continually teaches, reminds, and guides believers as they walk with God. Spiritual wisdom grows not only through isolated moments of insight but through daily attentiveness and responsiveness to the Spirit. Keeping in step with the Spirit means remaining sensitive to God's guidance in everyday decisions, attitudes, conversations, and priorities.

Discussion Questions:

1. Read Galatians 5:25. What does it mean to "keep in step with the Spirit"?

2. According to John 14:26, what role does the Holy Spirit play in the believer's life?

3. Why is spiritual wisdom closely connected to relationship with God?

4. How can believers become more attentive to the Spirit's guidance daily?

5. What distractions or habits can make it difficult to hear or follow God's wisdom?

KEY POINT 5: God's Wisdom Leads Us Through Relationship, Not Mere Information

Scriptures: Ephesians 1:17–18; Proverbs 3:5–6; James 1:5

Scripture Insights: Biblical wisdom is deeply relational. God's goal is not simply to give information but to deepen trust, dependence, and closeness with Him. As believers seek God through prayer, Scripture, wise counsel, and obedience, the eyes of their hearts become enlightened and they begin to discern God's wisdom more clearly over time.

Discussion Questions:

1. Read Ephesians 1:17–18. What kind of wisdom does Paul pray believers would receive?

2. Why is spiritual wisdom more relational than informational?

3. How does closeness with God affect discernment and decision-making?

4. Why does dependence often grow strongest during uncertain seasons?

5. What practical habit could help you stay closer to God and more sensitive to His wisdom?

F. SECTION 3: PERSONAL APPLICATION & REFLECTION

1. Where might God be inviting you to trust His wisdom instead of your own understanding?

2. What fear or pressure may be clouding your ability to discern God's direction?

3. How can you become more attentive to the Holy Spirit's guidance in daily life?

4. What is one next step of obedience or trust you sense God calling you to take this week?

G. CLOSING WISDOM KEYS

1. God's wisdom is revealed by the Spirit and received through humble dependence on Him.

2. Trusting God often means walking forward without having every answer in advance.

3. As believers stay close to God and walk in step with the Spirit,

wisdom unfolds faithfully over time.

H. PRAYER

I. PRAYER POINTS

1. Ask God to help you trust His wisdom more deeply than your own understanding.

2. Pray for patience and confidence in God's timing and guidance.

3. Present your current decisions, uncertainties, and burdens before God.

4. Ask the Holy Spirit to help you remain sensitive, attentive, and responsive to His leading.

Ask for individual prayer requests and pray for the individual needs of your group members and any area the Spirit directs.

II. CLOSING PRAYER

Heavenly Father, thank You that You are a God who gives wisdom generously to those who seek You. Teach us to trust You beyond our own understanding and to depend more fully on Your Spirit. Help us remain patient when answers seem delayed and faithful when the path ahead feels unclear. Guide our hearts, shape our thinking through Your Word, and help us walk step by step in alignment with Your wisdom and timing. Thank You for leading us faithfully even when we cannot yet see the full picture. In Jesus' name, Amen.

Use the Chapter 6 Daily Believer Declarations during the week.

KEY TRUTH TO REMEMBER

God's wisdom is revealed by the Spirit, received through trust, and walked out step by step as we stay close to Him.

The Secret of Spiritual Wisdom

Day 1 — Wisdom from God

Scripture: 1 Corinthians 2:7

Declaration: God reveals His wisdom to me by His Spirit. I depend on Him rather than my own understanding.

Prayer: Holy Spirit, help me receive the wisdom You freely give today. In Jesus' name. In Jesus' name. Amen.

Day 2 — Trusting God's Guidance

Scripture: Proverbs 3:5–6

Declaration: I trust the Lord with all my heart. As I submit my ways to Him, He directs my path.

Prayer: Father, I place my plans and decisions under Your leadership today. In Jesus' name. Amen.

Day 3 — Asking with Confidence

Scripture: James 1:5

Declaration: When I lack wisdom, I ask God and He gives generously. I am not afraid to depend on Him.

Prayer: God, thank You for inviting me to ask and receive Your wisdom. In Jesus' name. Amen.

Day 4 — Walking Step by Step

Scripture: Psalm 119:105

Declaration: God's Word is a lamp for my feet and a light for my path. I take the next faithful step with confidence.

Prayer: Lord Jesus, guide me with Your Word as I walk forward today. In Your name. Amen.

Day 5 — Led by the Spirit

Scripture: Galatians 5:25

Declaration: Since I live by the Spirit, I keep in step with the Spirit. God's wisdom guides me in every part of my life.

Prayer: Holy Spirit, help me stay attentive and responsive to Your leading. In Jesus' name. Amen.

Day 6 — God at Work Behind the Scenes

Scripture: Habakkuk 2:3

Declaration: God's plan is unfolding in His time—slowly, steadily, and surely. I trust His timing and remain patient.

Prayer: Father, help me trust You when progress feels slow. In Jesus' name. Amen.

Day 7 — Wisdom for Today

Scripture: John 16:13

Declaration: The Spirit of truth guides me into all truth. God gives me wisdom for each step I take.

Prayer: Lord Jesus, thank You for guiding me faithfully day by day. In Your name. Amen.

CHAPTER 7 STUDY GUIDE: THE SECRET OF CONTENTMENT

A. SESSION AIM

To help participants discover that contentment is learned through dependence on Christ rather than changing circumstances, and that Christ's sufficiency produces peace, stability, gratitude, and freedom from comparison and fear.

B. ICE BREAKER

What is something in life that brings peace or stability because it remains steady rather than constantly changing?

Leader Note: Encourage participants to think about dependable relationships, routines, or sources of stability. Help the group begin considering how spiritual contentment is rooted in what remains steady rather than what constantly shifts.

C. OPEN YOUR SESSION WITH PRAYER

Invite someone to open in prayer, or use the prayer below:

Heavenly Father, thank You that true peace and contentment are found in You. Quiet our restless hearts today and help us release fear, comparison, anxiety, and striving. Teach us to trust Your sufficiency and to rest in Your faithful care. Open our hearts to Your Word and strengthen us through Christ, who is enough in every season. In Jesus' nam e, Amen.

D. INTRODUCTION (CHAPTER 7 SUMMARY)

Every believer eventually faces seasons where peace feels fragile and contentment seems difficult to hold onto. Circumstances change, expectations go unmet, prayers seem delayed, and comparison quietly steals joy. Many people assume peace will come once life finally improves or becomes easier.

But Scripture reveals something very different. Contentment is not found in favorable circumstances—it is learned through dependence on Christ. The Bible presents contentment not as passive resignation or denial of reality, but as a steady confidence in God's sufficiency and presence.

The apostle Paul teaches that contentment grows as believers learn to rely on Christ's strength rather than their own ability or external conditions. As believers trust God's care, release comparison, and anchor themselves in Christ's sufficiency, peace begins to stabilize the heart even when life remains uncertain.

This chapter reminds us that contentment is not about controlling circumstances—it is about trusting Christ as our source within them.

E. BIBLE DISCUSSION

SECTION 1: PERSONALIZING THE MESSAGE

1. What kinds of circumstances most tend to disrupt your peace or contentment?

2. In what ways does comparison affect people emotionally and spiritually today?

3. Have you ever experienced a season where God taught you contentment through difficulty or waiting?

4. What area of your life currently requires deeper trust in God's

sufficiency?

SECTION 2: SCRIPTURE DISCOVERY

KEY POINT 1: Contentment Is Learned Through Dependence on Christ

Scriptures: Philippians 4:11–13; 2 Corinthians 3:5; Psalm 23:1

Scripture Insights: Paul teaches that contentment is not automatic—it is learned over time through dependence on Christ in every season of life. True sufficiency does not come from circumstances, personal ability, or control, but from God Himself. Contentment grows as believers shift the source of their peace from external conditions to God's faithful presence and provision.

Discussion Questions:

1. Read Philippians 4:11–13. What does Paul say about how contentment develops?

2. Why do you think contentment must be learned rather than assumed?

3. According to 2 Corinthians 3:5, where does true sufficiency come from?

4. How does Psalm 23:1 redefine what it means to "lack nothing"?

5. What circumstances most tempt you to rely on yourself instead of God?

KEY POINT 2: Christ's Strength Sustains Us in Every Season

Scriptures: Philippians 4:13; John 15:1–5; 2 Corinthians 12:9–10

Scripture Insights: Contentment is sustained not by changed circumstances but by Christ's strength within believers. Paul explains that Christ empowers him to remain steady through both abundance and hardship. Jesus teaches that spiritual life flows from remaining connected to Him like branches connected to a vine. God's grace becomes most visible in weakness as believers depend on Christ rather than themselves.

Discussion Questions:

1. Read Philippians 4:13 in context. What does Paul actually mean by "I can do all things through Christ"?

2. According to John 15:5, why is abiding in Christ essential for spiritual stability?

3. How does Christ's strength differ from self-reliance or emotional willpower?

4. Why does God sometimes choose to work through weakness instead of removing it immediately?

5. How can weakness become an opportunity for deeper dependence on Christ?

KEY POINT 3: Contentment Breaks the Power of Comparison and Fear

Scriptures: Hebrews 13:5–6; 1 Timothy 6:6–10; Psalm 23

Scripture Insights: Comparison and fear quietly destroy peace by convincing believers that they lack what they need or have been overlooked by God. Scripture teaches that contentment grows when believers anchor their confidence in God's presence rather than possessions, status, or external success. God's nearness becomes the foundation for peace, freedom, and security.

Discussion Questions:

1. Read Hebrews 13:5–6. What promise does God give that addresses fear and insecurity?

2. How does comparison quietly steal peace and joy?

3. According to 1 Timothy 6:6–10, what danger comes from

constantly desiring "more"?

4. Why does God's presence matter more than changing circumstances?

5. In what area of your life do you most need freedom from comparison or fear?

KEY POINT 4: Contentment Produces Stability, Gratitude, and Generosity

Scriptures: Proverbs 14:30; Ecclesiastes 4:6; Philippians 4:11–13

Scripture Insights: As contentment takes root in the heart, believers become steadier, more grateful, and less controlled by anxiety or striving. Contentment produces freedom from envy and the exhausting pursuit of more. Instead of reacting constantly to what is lacking, believers begin recognizing God's faithfulness and living with open-handed trust and generosity.

Discussion Questions:

1. According to Proverbs 14:30, what effect does envy have on the heart?

2. What does Ecclesiastes 4:6 teach about constant striving for more?

3. Why does gratitude naturally grow when contentment deepens?

4. How does contentment help believers become more generous and less fearful?

5. What practical habits can help cultivate gratitude and stability daily?

KEY POINT 5: True Peace Is Found in Christ's Sufficiency, Not Perfect Circumstances

Scriptures: Colossians 2:10; Psalm 23:1; Hebrews 13:5–6

Scripture Insights: Believers may still experience incomplete circumstances, unanswered questions, or difficult seasons, yet Scripture declares that they are already complete in Christ. Peace is not rooted in life becoming perfect but in trusting that Christ Himself is enough. Contentment grows as believers rest in God's faithful presence and care rather than waiting for ideal conditions.

Discussion Questions:

1. Read Colossians 2:10. What does it mean to be "complete in Christ"?

2. Why is it difficult to believe we already have what is most essential in Christ?

3. How does Psalm 23 shift the focus from circumstances to God's presence?

4. What difference exists between temporary comfort and true contentment?

5. How would your outlook change if you fully trusted Christ's sufficiency for this season?

F. SECTION 3: PERSONAL APPLICATION & REFLECTION

1. Where might God be inviting you to practice deeper contentment in this season?

2. What thought patterns, comparisons, or fears most often disturb your peace?

3. How can you become more aware of Christ's sufficiency in everyday life?

4. What practical step can you take this week to cultivate gratitude and trust instead of striving?

G. CLOSING WISDOM KEYS

1. Contentment is learned as believers depend on Christ rather

than changing circumstances.

2. Christ's strength sustains believers even when life remains difficult or uncertain.

3. Contentment frees the heart from comparison, fear, and constant striving for more.

H. PRAYER

I. PRAYER POINTS

1. Ask God to help you trust His sufficiency more deeply in every season of life.

2. Pray for freedom from comparison, anxiety, restlessness, and fear.

3. Present your current burdens, disappointments, and areas of struggle before God.

4. Ask the Holy Spirit to cultivate gratitude, stability, peace, and generosity within your heart.

Ask for individual prayer requests and pray for the individual needs of your group members and any area the Spirit directs.

II. CLOSING PRAYER

Heavenly Father, thank You that true contentment is found in You alone. Teach us to depend on Christ's strength instead of our own understanding or circumstances. Quiet every restless and anxious place within our hearts and help us trust Your faithful care. Free us from comparison, fear, and the endless pursuit of more. Let gratitude, peace, and steady trust grow within us as we learn to rest in Christ's sufficiency. Thank You that You are enough for every season of life. In Jesus' name, Amen.

Use the Chapter 7 Daily Believer Declarations during the week.

KEY TRUTH TO REMEMBER

Contentment is not found in changing circumstances, but in trusting Christ as our sufficiency.

DAILY BELIEVER DECLARATIONS (CHAPTER 7)

The Secret of Contentment

Day 1 — God Is Making His Will Known

Scripture: Ephesians 1:9

Declaration: God is making His will known to me as I walk with Him.

Wisdom Key: God delights in revealing His will to surrendered hearts.

Prayer: Father, thank You that Your will is not hidden from me. Help me walk closely with You today. In Jesus' name. Amen.

Day 2 — My Mind Is Being Renewed

Scripture: Romans 12:2

Declaration: My thinking is being renewed, and discernment is growing.

Wisdom Key: Transformation creates clarity.

Prayer: Lord Jesus, renew my mind so I can recognize what pleases You. In Jesus' name. Amen.

Day 3 — God Guides Me Through His Word

Scripture: Psalm 119:105

Declaration: God's Word lights my path one step at a time.

Wisdom Key: Scripture gives guidance even when the full path is unclear.

Prayer: Father God, guide me today through Your Word and truth. In Jesus' name. Amen.

Day 4 — I Ask God for Wisdom

Scripture: James 1:5

Declaration: I ask God for wisdom, and He gives generously.

Wisdom Key: Dependence invites revelation.

Prayer: Father God, I receive Your wisdom with humility and trust today. In Jesus' name. Amen.

Day 5 — God's Peace Guards My Decisions

Scripture: Colossians 3:15

Declaration: God's peace rules in my heart and guides my choices.

Wisdom Key: Peace is a sign of alignment with God's will.

Prayer: Holy Spirit, help me follow Your peace today. In Jesus' name. Amen.

Day 6 — God Uses Wise Counsel

Scripture: Proverbs 15:22

Declaration: God gives wisdom through godly counsel in my life.

Wisdom Key: Wise voices help confirm God's direction.

Prayer: Lord Jesus, thank You for people who help me walk wisely. In Jesus' name. Amen.

Day 7 — God Directs My Path

Scripture: Proverbs 16:3

Declaration: As I commit my ways to the Lord, He directs my steps.

Wisdom Key: Obedience opens the way for clarity.

Prayer: Father God, I entrust my plans to You and trust Your direction. In Jesus' name. Amen.

CHAPTER 8 STUDY GUIDE: THE SECRET OF GOD'S WILL

A. SESSION AIM

To help participants understand that God's will is discerned through relationship, renewed thinking, and spiritual wisdom rather than fear, pressure, or striving for certainty.

B. ICE BREAKER

What is a decision in life that required patience, trust, and gradual clarity rather than immediate answers?

Leader Note: Encourage honest but simple responses. Help participants begin thinking about how guidance often unfolds progressively rather than instantly.

C. OPEN YOUR SESSION WITH PRAYER

Invite someone to open in prayer, or use the prayer below:

Heavenly Father, thank You that You are not hiding Your will from Your people. Help us quiet fear, pressure, and anxiety as we seek Your wisdom today. Renew our minds through Your truth and teach us to trust You step by step. Open our hearts to hear Your Spirit and help us walk closely with You in every season. In Jesus' name, Amen.

D. INTRODUCTION (CHAPTER 8 SUMMARY)

Few questions trouble believers more deeply than wondering how to discern God's will. Many sincerely desire to follow God faithfully but feel pressure about making the wrong decision, missing God's plan, or misunderstanding His direction. As a result, God's will can begin to feel mysterious, fragile, or difficult to find.

But Scripture presents a far more comforting and relational picture. God's will is not a hidden code meant to frustrate believers. It is a revealed purpose centered on Christ and unfolded progressively through relationship, surrender, renewed thinking, and spiritual wisdom.

The Bible teaches that God guides willing hearts patiently and faithfully. Discernment grows not primarily through pressure or fear, but as believers remain close to God through Scripture, prayer, obedience, wise counsel, and attentiveness to the Holy Spirit. God's goal is not merely to help believers make correct decisions, but to form hearts that increasingly reflect His wisdom and trust His leadership.

This chapter reminds us that God is far more committed to guiding surrendered hearts than believers are capable of missing His will.

E. BIBLE DISCUSSION

SECTION 1: PERSONALIZING THE MESSAGE

1. What kinds of decisions or situations most make you anxious about God's will?

2. Why do you think many believers fear "missing" God's plan for their lives?

3. Have you ever experienced a season where clarity came gradually rather than instantly?

4. What area of your life currently requires greater trust in God's guidance?

SECTION 2: SCRIPTURE DISCOVERY

KEY POINT 1: God's Will Is Revealed Through Relationship

Scriptures: Ephesians 1:9–10; Psalm 25:14; John 14:21

Scripture Insights: Scripture teaches that God's will is not primarily discovered through pressure or analysis but revealed through relationship with Him. God delights in making His purposes known to hearts that walk closely with Him in humility, trust, and obedience. As believers deepen their relationship with God, discernment grows and His direction becomes clearer.

Discussion Questions:

1. Read Ephesians 1:9–10. What does Paul say about how God reveals His will?

2. How does centering God's will on Christ reshape the way we think about guidance and decisions?

3. According to Psalm 25:14, who does God "confide" in?

4. Why is relationship with God more important than merely gathering information?

5. How does obedience deepen clarity according to John 14:21?

KEY POINT 2: God's Will Becomes Clear as Our Minds Are Renewed

Scriptures: Romans 12:1–2; Ephesians 4:20–24

Scripture Insights: Discernment grows as believers surrender themselves to God and allow the Holy Spirit to renew their thinking. Transformation changes how believers see life, evaluate decisions, and respond to God's guidance. God's will becomes increasingly discernible as worldly patterns lose influence and the mind becomes shaped by Scripture and God's truth.

Discussion Questions:

1. Read Romans 12:1–2. According to Paul, what comes before discernment?

2. Why does surrender matter in recognizing God's will?

3. How does renewing the mind affect decision-making and spiritual clarity?

4. According to Ephesians 4:20–24, what old patterns or mindsets may hinder discernment?

5. What areas of your thinking may need greater renewal through God's truth?

KEY POINT 3: God Gives Wisdom Generously to Those Who Ask

Scriptures: James 1:5; Colossians 1:9

Scripture Insights: God does not withhold wisdom from sincere believers. Scripture teaches that wisdom is a gift generously given by God through the Spirit. Spiritual wisdom grows through prayer, humility, attentiveness, and dependence on God rather than self-reliance. God faithfully guides willing hearts through Spirit-given wisdom and understanding.

Discussion Questions:

1. Read James 1:5. What does this verse teach about God's character?

2. Why do people sometimes hesitate to ask God for wisdom?

3. According to Colossians 1:9, what kind of wisdom does Paul pray believers would receive?

4. Why is spiritual wisdom different from merely having information or intelligence?

5. How can believers become more dependent on God's wisdom

in daily life?

KEY POINT 4: God Guides Step by Step Through Trust and Obedience

Scriptures: Proverbs 3:5–6; Habakkuk 2:3; Proverbs 16:3

Scripture Insights: God often guides believers progressively rather than revealing everything at once. Wisdom unfolds as believers trust God beyond their own understanding and walk faithfully in what He has already revealed. Obedience clarifies direction over time. God's timing may feel slow, but His guidance is always purposeful, wise, and trustworthy.

Discussion Questions:

1. Read Proverbs 3:5–6. What does it mean to trust God rather than lean on your own understanding?

2. Why is waiting often difficult in the process of discernment?

3. According to Habakkuk 2:3, what does God's timing teach us about patience and trust?

4. How does obedience help bring greater clarity over time?

5. What situation in your life currently requires trusting God step by step?

KEY POINT 5: God's Peace and Spirit Help Guide Believers in Discernment

Scriptures: Colossians 3:15; Philippians 4:6–7; Galatians 5:25

Scripture Insights: As believers walk closely with God, the Holy Spirit provides peace, wisdom, and guidance. God's peace often confirms alignment with His character and truth, while ongoing confusion, fear, or striving may signal the need to pause and seek greater clarity. Spiritual discernment grows as believers remain attentive and responsive to the Spirit's leading.

Discussion Questions:

1. Read Colossians 3:15. How does the peace of Christ help guide believers?

2. According to Philippians 4:6–7, what happens when believers bring anxiety to God in prayer?

3. Why is inner peace different from simply avoiding difficulty?

4. What might disrupt spiritual peace during decision-making?

5. How can believers "keep in step with the Spirit" practically in everyday life?

F. SECTION 3: PERSONAL APPLICATION & REFLECTION

1. Where might God be inviting you to trust Him more deeply right now?

2. Which patterns of discernment have helped you recognize God's wisdom in the past? (For example: Scripture, prayer, wise counsel, peace, obedience, or circumstances.)

3. Which area of discernment do you sense you most need to grow in during this season?

4. What practical step can you take this week to stay closer to God and more attentive to His guidance?

G. CLOSING WISDOM KEYS

1. God's will is revealed relationally as believers walk closely with Him.

2. Discernment grows as minds are renewed and hearts are surrendered to God.

3. God faithfully guides willing hearts through spiritual wisdom, peace, and obedience step by step.

H. PRAYER

I. PRAYER POINTS

1. Ask God to help you trust His guidance instead of fear or pressure.

2. Pray for renewed thinking and greater sensitivity to the Holy Spirit.

3. Present your current decisions, uncertainties, and questions before God.

4. Ask the Holy Spirit for wisdom, peace, and faithful obedience as you walk forward.

Ask for individual prayer requests and pray for the individual needs of your group members and any area the Spirit directs.

II. CLOSING PRAYER

Heavenly Father, thank You that Your will is not hidden from surrendered hearts. Help us trust You more deeply and release the fear of missing Your plan. Renew our minds through Your truth and teach us to walk closely with You in humility, wisdom, and obedience. Give us peace when life feels uncertain and help us recognize Your guidance step by step. Thank You for faithfully leading us according to Your good purpose in Christ. In Jesus' name, Amen.

Use the Chapter 8 Daily Believer Declarations during the week.

KEY TRUTH TO REMEMBER

God's will is not hidden from surrendered hearts; it becomes clear as we walk closely with Him.

The Secret of God's Will

Day 1 — Relationship

Scripture: Psalm 25:14; John 14:21

Declaration: I walk closely with God, and He reveals His heart to me. As I grow in relationship with Him, His will becomes clearer in my life.

Prayer: Father God, draw me closer to You today. Help me to walk with You in trust and obedience so I can know Your heart and follow Your ways. In Jesus' name. Amen.

Day 2 — Renewed Mind

Scripture: Romans 12:1–2; Ephesians 4:23

Declaration: My mind is being renewed by God's truth. As my thinking changes, I am able to discern and walk in God's will.

Prayer: Lord Jesus, renew my mind today. Help me see life from Your perspective and align my thoughts with Your truth. In Your name. A men.

Day 3 — God's Will

Scripture: Ephesians 1:9–10; Proverbs 3:5–6

Declaration: God's will is not hidden from me. He is faithfully guiding my life according to His purpose in Christ.

Prayer: Father God, I trust Your plan for my life. Lead me step by step and help me walk confidently in Your will. In Jesus' name. Amen.

Day 4 — Trust

Scripture: Proverbs 3:5–6; Isaiah 30:21

Declaration: I trust God with all my heart. Even when I don't understand, I know He is directing my steps.

Prayer: Lord Jesus, help me trust You beyond what I can see. Teach me to rely on Your wisdom instead of my own understanding. In Your name. A men.

Day 5 — Spiritual Wisdom

Scripture: Colossians 1:9; James 1:5

Declaration: God fills me with wisdom through His Spirit. I have insight and understanding for every decision I face.

Prayer: Holy Spirit, fill me with Your wisdom today. Help me listen carefully and respond faithfully to Your leading. In Jesus' name. Amen.

Day 6 — Step-by-Step Guidance

Scripture: Psalm 119:105; Habakkuk 2:3

Declaration: God guides me step by step. I do not need to see the whole path—I trust Him to lead me faithfully.

Prayer: Father God, thank You for guiding me each day. Help me walk in the light You give and trust You with what I cannot yet see. In Jesus' name. Amen.

Day 7 — Thanksgiving & Peace

Scripture: Philippians 4:6–7; Colossians 3:15

Declaration: God's peace guards my heart as I trust Him. I am grateful for His guidance, His presence, and His faithful direction in my life.

Prayer: Thank You, Lord Jesus, for guiding me with wisdom and peace. I choose to trust You and rest in Your faithful care. In Jesus' name. Amen.

CHAPTER 9 STUDY GUIDE: THE SECRET OF TRANSFORMATION

A. SESSION AIM

To help participants understand that spiritual transformation is not driven by pressure or self-effort, but unfolds progressively through relationship with God, secure identity in Christ, and continual yielding to the Holy Spirit.

This session invites participants to rest in God's process of change—discovering that while salvation happens in a moment, transformation unfolds over time as the Spirit forms Christ's life within us.

B. ICE BREAKER

When you think about "change," do you tend to picture pressure and effort—or growth and process? Why do you think that is?

Leader Note: Keep this relaxed and reflective. Encourage honesty without trying to correct responses. The goal is simply to help participants recognize how they naturally think about growth and transformation.

C. OPEN YOUR SESSION WITH PRAYER

Invite someone to open in prayer, or use the prayer below:

Heavenly Father, thank You that transformation is Your work within us. Help us release pressure, fear, and striving as we learn to trust Your Spirit more deeply. Open our hearts to receive Your truth today and help us remain surrendered to the process of change You are faithfully working in us. In Jesus' name, Amen.

D. INTRODUCTION (CHAPTER 9 SUMMARY)

One of the most discouraging tensions in the Christian life is the gap between what believers know to be true and what they still experience in daily life. Many sincerely love God and desire to grow, yet still wrestle with old patterns, weakness, inconsistency, and slow progress. Over time, this struggle can create frustration, shame, or anxiety about spiritual g rowth.

But Scripture presents transformation very differently than many expect. Transformation is not instant perfection, behavior management, or self-improvement. It is a Spirit-led process rooted in God's revealed truth and sustained through relationship with Him. God is not merely changing behavior—He is forming Christ's life within believers.

The Bible teaches that transformation begins with revelation, deepens as believers behold Christ, grows from secure identity rather than fear, and is sustained through continual yielding to the Holy Spirit. Struggle does not mean transformation has failed. Often, it reveals that transformation is actively underway.

This chapter reminds us that believers are not transforming themselves—they are being transformed by the Spirit as they remain turned toward Christ.

E. BIBLE DISCUSSION

SECTION 1: PERSONALIZING THE MESSAGE

1. What parts of spiritual growth feel most frustrating or discouraging to you sometimes?

2. Why do many believers expect transformation to happen faster

than it often does?

3. Have you ever experienced a season where growth became visible only in hindsight?

4. What area of your life currently requires greater patience with God's process of transformation?

SECTION 2: SCRIPTURE DISCOVERY

KEY POINT 1: Transformation Begins with Revelation, Not Self-Improvement

Scriptures: Romans 16:25–26; 2 Corinthians 3:18

Scripture Insights: Transformation begins when believers receive and respond to the truth God has revealed in Christ. Scripture teaches that spiritual growth is not rooted in self-effort or behavior management but in revelation—seeing more clearly who Christ is and who believers are in Him. As believers behold Christ, the Spirit steadily reshapes them from the inside out.

Discussion Questions:

1. Read Romans 16:25–26. What does Paul say God has now revealed through the gospel?

2. Why is transformation more than simply modifying behavior?

3. According to 2 Corinthians 3:18, who is responsible for transformation?

4. What does it mean to "behold" or "contemplate" the Lord's glory?

5. How can staying focused on Christ reshape the way believers grow spiritually?

KEY POINT 2: Transformation Is Progressive, Not Instant

Scriptures: Philippians 1:6; 2 Corinthians 3:18; Galatians 5:25

Scripture Insights: Scripture consistently presents transformation as an ongoing process rather than instant perfection. God faithfully continues the work He begins within believers, shaping them over time through the Holy Spirit. Growth may sometimes feel slow, but God is patient, purposeful, and fully committed to completing His work.

Discussion Questions:

1. Read Philippians 1:6. What confidence does Paul express about God's work in believers?

2. Why do believers often become discouraged during slow seasons of growth?

3. How does understanding transformation as a process relieve unnecessary pressure?

4. According to Galatians 5:25, what does it mean to "keep in step with the Spirit"?

5. What evidence of gradual growth have you seen in your life over time?

KEY POINT 3: Transformation Flows from Identity, Not Fear

Scriptures: Romans 8:1; Romans 8:15; 2 Corinthians 5:17

Scripture Insights: Transformation grows best in the environment of secure identity and grace rather than fear and condemnation. Believers are not trying to earn acceptance with God—they are learning to live from the identity already given to them in Christ. The Holy Spirit produces assurance, sonship, and freedom rather than anxiety-driven striving.

Discussion Questions:

1. Read Romans 8:15. What contrast does Paul make between fear and adoption?

2. Why is fear often harmful to spiritual growth?

3. According to 2 Corinthians 5:17, what has already become true about believers in Christ?

4. How does secure identity help believers face struggle without shame?

5. What fears or insecurities most tempt you to strive instead of rest in God's grace?

KEY POINT 4: Transformation Is Sustained Through Daily Yielding to the Spirit

Scriptures: Galatians 5:16; Galatians 5:25; Philippians 2:12–13

Scripture Insights: Transformation is sustained through ongoing responsiveness to the Holy Spirit. Believers actively participate in growth by yielding daily to God's work within them. Scripture teaches that God supplies both the desire and the power for transformation, while believers respond through obedience, attentiveness, and surrendered living.

Discussion Questions:

1. Read Philippians 2:12–13. What balance do you see between God's work and human participation?

2. What does daily yielding to the Spirit practically look like?

3. How is yielding different from passivity or striving?

4. According to Galatians 5:16, what happens as believers walk by the Spirit?

5. What area of your life currently requires greater surrender to the Holy Spirit?

KEY POINT 5: Transformation Produces New Ways of Thinking and Living

Scriptures: Ephesians 4:22–24; John 15:4–5

Scripture Insights: The Spirit renews believers from the inside out by reshaping their thinking, desires, and responses. Transformation involves putting off old patterns, allowing the mind to be renewed, and learning to live from the new identity already given in Christ. As believers remain connected to Christ, spiritual fruit naturally grows over time.

Discussion Questions:

Read Ephesians 4:22–24. What three movements of transformation does Paul describe?

1. Why is renewing the mind essential for lasting change?

2. According to John 15:4–5, why is abiding in Christ necessary for fruitfulness?

3. How does spiritual growth differ from simply trying harder?

4. What old pattern or mindset may God currently be inviting you to release?

F. SECTION 3: PERSONAL APPLICATION & REFLECTION

1. Which part of transformation feels most challenging for you right now?

2. Where do you sense God inviting you to release pressure and trust His process more deeply?

3. What would daily yielding to the Spirit look like in your current season?

4. What practical step can you take this week to remain more intentionally connected to Christ?

G. CLOSING WISDOM KEYS

1. Transformation begins with revelation and relationship, not self-improvement or pressure.

2. Spiritual growth unfolds progressively as believers behold

Christ and remain surrendered to the Spirit.

3. Secure identity in Christ creates the environment where genuine transformation can grow steadily over time.

H. PRAYER

I. PRAYER POINTS

1. Ask God to help you trust His process of transformation rather than striving in your own strength.

2. Pray for freedom from fear, shame, condemnation, and comparison.

3. Present areas of struggle, weakness, or discouragement before God honestly.

4. Ask the Holy Spirit to help you remain surrendered, attentive, and responsive to His leading daily.

Ask for individual prayer requests and pray for the individual needs of your group members and any area the Spirit directs.

II. CLOSING PRAYER

Heavenly Father, thank You that transformation is Your faithful work within us. Help us stop striving to change ourselves through pressure and instead remain connected to Christ through trust and surrender. Remind us that we are Your children, secure in Your love and free from condemnation. Teach us to walk daily in step with the Holy Spirit and to trust Your process even when growth feels slow. Thank You that You are patiently forming Christ's life within us one step at a time. In Jesus' name, Amen.

Use the Chapter 9 Daily Believer Declarations during the week.

KEY TRUTH TO REMEMBER

Transformation is not instant perfection, but a Spirit-led process of becoming more like Christ as we remain surrendered to Him.

The Secret of Transformation

Day 1 — Transformation Begins with Turning to the Lord

Scripture: *"And we all, who with unveiled faces contemplate the Lord's glory, are being transformed into His image with ever-increasing glory, which comes from the Lord, who is the Spirit."* — 2 Corinthians 3:18 (NIV)

Declaration: I turn my heart toward the Lord, and as I behold Him, He transforms me.

Wisdom Key: Transformation begins not with striving, but with staying present to God.

Prayer: Holy Spirit, I turn my attention toward You today. Help me to behold the Lord's glory with an open and unveiled heart. As I stay present with You, continue Your transforming work in me. I trust You to shape me from the inside out. In Jesus' name. Amen.

Day 2 — Transformation Is the Work of the Spirit

Scripture: *"We... are being transformed... which comes from the Lord, who is the Spirit."* — 2 Corinthians 3:18 (NIV)

Declaration: I do not transform myself; the Spirit of the Lord is transforming me.

Wisdom Key: What God initiates by grace, He sustains by His Spirit.

Prayer: Father God, thank You that transformation is Your work, not mine to force. I release self-effort and receive Your grace today. Holy Spirit, continue shaping my heart, my mind, and my life according to Your will. In Jesus' name. Amen.

Day 3 — Transformation Is Progressive, Not Instant

Scripture: *"Being confident of this, that He who began a good work in you will carry it on to completion."* — Philippians 1:6 (NIV)

Declaration: God is faithfully completing His work in me, step by step.

Wisdom Key: Slow growth does not mean stalled growth—it often means deep formation.

Prayer: Lord Jesus, thank You for Your patience with my process. Help me trust You in seasons when growth feels slow or unseen. I rest in Your faithfulness, knowing You will complete what You have begun in me. In Your name. Amen.

Day 4 — Transformation Flows from Identity, Not Fear

Scripture: *"The Spirit you received does not make you slaves, so that you live in fear again; rather, the Spirit you received brought about your adoption to sonship."* — Romans 8:15 (NIV)

Declaration: I am God's child, and I grow from security, not fear.

Wisdom Key: Identity settled in love creates freedom for lasting change.

Prayer: Abba Father, thank You that I belong to You. I renounce fear-driven striving and receive the assurance of my adoption. Let my growth flow from knowing I am loved, accepted, and secure in You. In Jesus' name. Amen.

Day 5 — There Is No Condemnation in My Growth

Scripture: *"Therefore, there is now no condemnation for those who are in*

Christ Jesus." — Romans 8:1 (NIV)

Declaration: I grow under grace, not condemnation.

Wisdom Key: Grace creates space for honesty, healing, and transformation.

Prayer: Lord Jesus, thank You that I am not growing under judgment, but under grace. Quiet every voice of shame and accusation. Help me walk forward in freedom, knowing You are for me as You shape my life. In Your name. Amen.

Day 6 — I Remain in Christ and Bear Fruit

Scripture: *"Remain in Me, as I also remain in you... If you remain in Me and I in you, you will bear much fruit."* — John 15:4–5 (NIV)

Declaration: As I remain in Christ, His life produces fruit in me.

Wisdom Key: Fruit grows naturally where connection is maintained.

Prayer: Lord Jesus, I choose to remain in You today. Help me stay connected to Your presence, Your Word, and Your Spirit. I trust that as I abide in You, Your life will bear fruit through me. In Your name. Amen.

Day 7 — Transformation Is Sustained by Continual Yielding

Scripture: *"Since we live by the Spirit, let us keep in step with the Spirit."* — Galatians 5:25 (NIV)

Declaration: I keep in step with the Spirit through daily yielding.

Wisdom Key: Transformation is sustained by willingness and posture, not willpower.

Prayer: Holy Spirit, I yield myself to You today. I choose to walk at Your pace, follow Your lead, and trust Your guidance. Continue forming Christ's life within me as I surrender one step at a time. In Jesus' name. A men.

CHAPTER 10 STUDY GUIDE: THE SECRET OF ENDURANCE IN SUFFERING

A. SESSION AIM

To help participants understand that endurance in suffering is not sustained by willpower or silence, but by dependence on God's grace, Christ's presence within us, and the hope that God is still at work even when pain and answers linger.

B. ICE BREAKER

What is something in life that requires endurance rather than quick strength (for example, recovery, long-distance travel, raising children, or learning a skill)? What helps you keep going?

Leader Note: Keep this light and conversational. Avoid trying to solve or advise one another. The goal is simply to recognize that meaningful growth and endurance usually develop gradually over time.

C. OPEN YOUR SESSION WITH PRAYER

Invite someone to open in prayer, or use the prayer below:

Heavenly Father, thank You that You are near to us in suffering and faithful in every season. Quiet anxious hearts, comfort those who are weary, and remind us that You are still at work even when answers seem delayed. Help us lean on Your grace instead of our own strength and guide our discussion today with Your presence and peace. In Jesus' name, Amen.

D. INTRODUCTION (CHAPTER 10 SUMMARY)

One of the hardest experiences in the Christian life is continuing to trust God when pain lingers and answers do not come quickly. Many believers sincerely love God yet still find themselves walking through loss, weakness, waiting, disappointment, or suffering that feels unresolved. In those moments, it becomes easy to wonder whether suffering means God is distant, displeased, or no longer working.

But Scripture reveals something profoundly different. Endurance is not emotional toughness or silent resignation—it is a Spirit-sustained work of grace. God does not abandon His people in suffering. He works within suffering to form endurance, deepen character, strengthen hope, refine faith, and draw believers into deeper dependence on Christ.

The Bible teaches that suffering is not wasted when entrusted to God. Christ's presence within believers becomes the source of strength, hope, and perseverance even when circumstances remain difficult. God may not always remove suffering immediately, but He faithfully sustains believers within it and uses it to form what will endure.

This chapter reminds us that endurance is not about escaping hardship, but about discovering God's sustaining presence and grace one faithful step at a time.

E. BIBLE DISCUSSION

SECTION 1: PERSONALIZING THE MESSAGE

1. What kinds of suffering or hardship most tend to test your faith and endurance?

2. Why do you think suffering often creates feelings of discouragement or confusion?

3. Have you ever experienced a season where God strengthened or shaped you through difficulty?

4. What truth about God do you most need to hold onto in your current season?

SECTION 2: SCRIPTURE DISCOVERY

KEY POINT 1: God Uses Suffering to Form Endurance, Character, and Hope

Scriptures: Romans 5:3–5; James 1:2–4

Scripture Insights: Scripture teaches that suffering is not meaningless when entrusted to God. Through hardship, God forms endurance, strengthens character, and deepens hope within believers. Endurance is not emotional toughness but Spirit-given faithfulness that continues trusting God even when relief is delayed. God uses suffering not to destroy faith but to mature and strengthen it.

Discussion Questions:

1. Read Romans 5:3–5. What progression does Paul describe in this passage?

2. How does this passage challenge the belief that suffering is meaningless or wasted?

3. According to James 1:2–4, what does perseverance ultimately produce?

4. Why is endurance different from simply "surviving" hardship?

5. What areas of your character or faith has suffering shaped most deeply?

KEY POINT 2: Endurance Grows as We Keep Our Eyes on Jesus

Scriptures: Hebrews 12:2–3; Colossians 1:26–27; Isaiah 41:10

Scripture Insights: Endurance is sustained when believers continually return their focus to Christ rather than becoming consumed by pain or discouragement. Jesus endured suffering faithfully and now walks with believers through their suffering. Christ's presence within believers becomes the source of hope, strength, and stability even when circumstances remain difficult.

Discussion Questions:

Read Hebrews 12:2–3. What does this passage encourage believers to do when they feel weary?

Why is focus so important during seasons of suffering?

According to Colossians 1:27, what hope sustains believers?

How does Isaiah 41:10 reassure believers during difficult seasons?

What practical ways can believers "fix their eyes on Jesus" daily?

KEY POINT 3: God Refines Faith Through Suffering, Not Punishes His Children

Scriptures: Job 23:10; Hebrews 12:10–11; 1 Peter 1:6–7

Scripture Insights: Scripture describes suffering as a refining process rather than rejection or punishment. God uses hardship to purify faith, deepen dependence, and form spiritual maturity within His people. Like gold refined through fire, believers are strengthened and shaped through trials that reveal and deepen genuine faith.

Discussion Questions:

1. Read Job 23:10. What confidence does Job express in the middle of suffering?

2. According to Hebrews 12:10–11, what purpose does God have in hardship?

3. Why is refinement different from punishment or rejection?

4. How does 1 Peter 1:6–7 describe the effect of trials on faith?

5. What encouragement comes from knowing God is purposeful and present in suffering?

KEY POINT 4: Endurance Is Sustained Through Dependence on God's Grace

Scriptures: Colossians 1:28–29; 2 Corinthians 12:9; Philippians 4:13

Scripture Insights: Believers are not called to endure suffering through self-reliance or sheer determination. Scripture teaches that endurance is sustained by God's grace and Christ's strength working within believers. Weakness becomes a place where God's power is displayed most clearly as believers continually lean on His sustaining presence.

Discussion Questions:

1. Read Colossians 1:28–29. What does Paul identify as the true source of his endurance?

2. According to 2 Corinthians 12:9, how does God respond to human weakness?

3. Why is weakness not a disqualification for spiritual growth?

4. How does Philippians 4:13 change the way believers view endurance?

5. What might it practically look like to "lean again" on God's grace this week?

KEY POINT 5: God's Grace Sustains Hope Even When Answers Linger

Scriptures: 2 Corinthians 4:16–18; Romans 8:18; 1 Peter 5:10

Scripture Insights: Scripture teaches that present suffering is temporary compared to the eternal glory God is preparing for believers. Even when answers are delayed and pain remains unresolved, God continues renewing believers inwardly and sustaining hope through His promises. Suffering is not the end of the story—God is still restoring, strengthening, and preparing what will endure.

Discussion Questions:

1. Read 2 Corinthians 4:16–18. What contrast does Paul make between outward suffering and inward renewal?

2. How does eternal perspective help believers endure present hardship?

3. According to Romans 8:18, how does future glory compare with present suffering?

4. What hope does 1 Peter 5:10 offer weary believers?

5. How can believers continue trusting God when answers remain delayed?

F. SECTION 3: PERSONAL APPLICATION & REFLECTION

1. Where do you most need reassurance that your suffering is not wasted?

2. What fears, disappointments, or burdens may God be inviting you to release into His care?

3. How might God be inviting you to depend more deeply on His grace instead of your own strength?

4. What would one faithful step of endurance look like for you this week?

G. CLOSING WISDOM KEYS

1. God uses suffering to form endurance, strengthen character, and deepen hope within believers.

2. Endurance grows not through self-reliance but through dependence on Christ's sustaining grace.

3. Suffering is not the end of the story—God is still at work, refining faith and forming what will endure.

H. PRAYER

I. PRAYER POINTS

1. Ask God to strengthen weary hearts and help you endure through dependence on His grace.

2. Pray for comfort, healing, and hope for those carrying pain, loss, unanswered questions, or discouragement.

3. Present your fears, burdens, disappointments, and weaknesses honestly before God.

4. Ask the Holy Spirit to renew your hope, deepen your trust, and help you remain faithful one day at a time.

Ask for individual prayer requests and pray for the individual needs of your group members and any area the Spirit directs.

II. CLOSING PRAYER

Heavenly Father, thank You that You remain near to us even in suffering. Thank You that our pain is not wasted and that You are faithfully at work within us even when answers feel delayed. Strengthen us through Your grace when our own strength feels depleted. Help us keep our eyes fixed on Jesus and trust that You are forming endurance, character, and hope within us. Comfort weary hearts, renew discouraged souls, and remind us that suffering is not the end of the story because You are still writing it with grace, faithfulness, and redemption. In Jesus' name, Amen.

Use the Chapter 10 Daily Believer Declarations during the week.

KEY TRUTH TO REMEMBER

Endurance in suffering is not sustained by willpower, but by dependence on God's grace, Christ's presence within us, and the hope that God is still at work even when pain lingers.

The Secret of Endurance in Suffering

Day 1 — God Is at Work Even When I Am Weak

Scripture: 2 Corinthians 4:16–18

Declaration: God is renewing me inwardly even when outward circumstances feel heavy.

Wisdom Key: What God is doing within me is more lasting than what I see around me.

Prayer: Father God, when I feel worn down, remind me that You are still at work in me. Renew my heart with hope and help me trust what You are forming beyond what I can see. In Jesus' name. Amen.

Day 2 — My Suffering Is Not Wasted

Scripture: Romans 5:3–5

Declaration: God is using this season to form endurance, shape my character, and strengthen my hope.

Wisdom Key: Suffering entrusted to God becomes a place of formation, not defeat.

Prayer: Lord, help me trust that this season is not meaningless. Even when the process is hard, I believe You are forming something that will endure. In Jesus' name. Amen.

Day 3 — I Fix My Eyes on Jesus

Scripture: Hebrews 12:2–3

Declaration: As I fix my eyes on Jesus, He steadies my heart and gives me strength to endure.

Wisdom Key: Endurance grows when my focus returns to Christ, not my circumstances.

Prayer: Jesus, help me lift my eyes to You when weariness sets in. Steady my heart and remind me that You walk with me through this season. In Jesus' name. Amen.

Day 4 — God Is Refining My Faith, Not Punishing Me

Scripture: Hebrews 12:10–11; Job 23:10

Declaration: God is refining my faith with care and purpose, shaping what will last.

Wisdom Key: Refinement is a sign of God's care, not His rejection.

Prayer: Father, when pain feels confusing, help me remember that You are refining, not rejecting me. Shape my faith and deepen my trust in You. In Jesus' name. Amen.

Day 5 — Christ Lives in Me and Sustains Me

Scripture: Colossians 1:26–29

Declaration: Christ lives in me and supplies the strength I need to endure.

Wisdom Key: Endurance is sustained by Christ within me, not by strength I produce.

Prayer: Lord Jesus, thank You that You live within me. When I feel depleted, help me rely on Your strength at work in my life. In Jesus' name. A men.

Day 6 — God's Grace Meets Me in My Weakness

Scripture: 2 Corinthians 12:9

Declaration: God's grace is sufficient for me, and His power meets me in my weakness.

Wisdom Key: Weakness is not the end of God's work—it is often where His power is revealed.

Prayer: God, I bring You my weakness today. Thank You that Your grace is enough and that You meet me with strength when I feel most limited. In Jesus' name. Amen.

Day 7 — I Lean on God's Strength, Not My Own

Scripture: Philippians 4:13

Declaration: I endure this season through Christ who strengthens me.

Wisdom Key: Endurance is sustained by dependence, not determination.

Prayer: Father, I release self-reliance and lean fully on You today. Strengthen me by Your Spirit and carry me forward one step at a time. In Jesus' name. Amen.

Chapter 11 Study Guide: The Secret of Faithfulness to the End

A. SESSION AIM

To help participants understand that faithfulness in God's Kingdom is measured by trustworthiness, sustained by hope, and rewarded by God over time—even when progress feels slow, hidden, or unseen.

B. ICE BREAKER

What is something in life that requires consistency over time rather than quick results (for example: health, relationships, raising children, learning a skill, or building trust)?

Leader Note: Keep responses simple and practical. Help participants begin thinking about the value of steady faithfulness over time rather than instant success or visible results.

C. OPEN YOUR SESSION WITH PRAYER

Invite someone to open in prayer, or use the prayer below:

Heavenly Father, thank You for Your faithfulness toward us. Quiet every anxious and weary heart today and help us trust You for the long journey. Teach us to remain steady in obedience, faithful in small things, and anchored in hope when results feel delayed. Guide our discussion with

Your wisdom and strengthen us to walk faithfully with You one step at a time. In Jesus' name, Amen.

D. INTRODUCTION (CHAPTER 11 SUMMARY)

One of the greatest challenges in the Christian life is remaining faithful when progress feels slow, hidden, or unnoticed. Many believers begin their journey with excitement, clarity, and conviction, but over time weariness can quietly settle in. The pressure to see visible fruit, measurable success, or recognition often creates discouragement when obedience feels repetitive or ordinary.

But Scripture reveals that God measures faithfulness differently than the world does. In God's Kingdom, faithfulness is not defined by speed, visibility, or impressiveness—it is defined by trustworthiness, steady obedience, and hope-filled perseverance over time.

The Bible consistently teaches that what God values most is often formed quietly. Character grows through repeated obedience in ordinary places. Faithfulness in small things becomes preparation for greater responsibility. And hope in Christ anchors believers through long seasons when fruit or reward feels delayed.

This chapter reminds us that faithfulness is not anxious striving for approval but steady trust in a faithful God who sees, remembers, and honors what is done in love and obedience.

E. BIBLE DISCUSSION

SECTION 1: PERSONALIZING THE MESSAGE

1. What kinds of situations most tempt you to become discouraged or impatient in your faith journey?

2. Why do you think people often equate visibility or results with value?

3. Have you ever experienced a season where quiet faithfulness later proved deeply meaningful?

4. What area of your life currently requires steady endurance and

trust in God's timing?

SECTION 2: SCRIPTURE DISCOVERY

KEY POINT 1: Faithfulness Is Stewardship, Not Self-Importance

Scriptures: 1 Corinthians 4:1–2; 1 Peter 4:10; James 1:17

Scripture Insights: Scripture teaches that believers are stewards of what God has entrusted to them. Faithfulness is not about impressiveness, recognition, or controlling outcomes—it is about trustworthiness with God's gifts, responsibilities, and opportunities. God values steady stewardship and humble obedience more than visibility or applause.

Discussion Questions:

1. Read 1 Corinthians 4:1–2. How does Paul describe the role of believers?

2. What does God require of those entrusted with responsibility?

3. According to 1 Peter 4:10, why has God given believers gifts and opportunities?

4. How does understanding stewardship relieve pressure about results or recognition?

5. What responsibilities or opportunities has God entrusted to you in this season?

KEY POINT 2: God Rewards Faithfulness Over Time

Scriptures: Matthew 25:21; Hebrews 10:32–36; Colossians 3:23–24

Scripture Insights: Scripture reassures believers that faithfulness is never wasted, even when results feel delayed or unseen. God sees quiet obedience, steady endurance, and hidden sacrifice. The reward of faithfulness is not merely future recognition but deeper fellowship with God, growing trust, and eternal significance rooted in His timing and wisdom.

Discussion Questions:

1. Read Matthew 25:21. What does the master commend in this passage?

2. According to Hebrews 10:32–36, what kinds of pressures were these believers enduring?

3. Why is perseverance often difficult during long seasons of obedience?

4. How does Colossians 3:23–24 reshape the way believers approach ordinary responsibilities?

5. What encouragement comes from knowing that God sees and remembers faithful obedience?

KEY POINT 3: Faithfulness in Small Things Shapes Character for Greater Responsibility

Scriptures: Luke 16:10; Luke 19:17; 1 Samuel 17:15

Scripture Insights: God often shapes believers through small, ordinary, and unseen acts of obedience before entrusting greater responsibility. Quiet faithfulness forms integrity, humility, perseverance, and dependence on God. What seems insignificant to people often becomes deeply significant in God's Kingdom because character is formed in repeated, steady obedience.

Discussion Questions:

1. Read Luke 16:10. Why do small acts of faithfulness matter to God?

2. According to Luke 19:17, what connection exists between small faithfulness and greater responsibility?

3. What do you notice about David's hidden years in 1 Samuel 17:15?

4. Why does God often use ordinary or repetitive seasons to shape

character?

5. What "small" area of faithfulness might God currently be using to shape you?

KEY POINT 4: Hope in Christ Sustains Faithfulness Through Long Seasons

Scriptures: Hebrews 6:19; Romans 8:25; Galatians 6:9

Scripture Insights: Faithfulness is sustained by hope anchored in Christ rather than pressure, hurry, or immediate results. Biblical hope steadies believers during long seasons of waiting and keeps them from drifting into discouragement or impatience. God's timing is purposeful, and hope allows believers to continue trusting Him even when progress feels hidden.

Discussion Questions:

1. Read Hebrews 6:19. How does hope function as an anchor for the soul?

2. Why is waiting often difficult for believers?

3. According to Romans 8:25, what relationship exists between hope and patience?

4. How does Galatians 6:9 encourage believers not to grow weary?

5. What area of your life currently requires greater patience and hope in God's timing?

KEY POINT 5: God Sees and Honors Faithfulness Done in Love

Scriptures: Hebrews 6:10; Matthew 6:4; Psalm 18:25

Scripture Insights: God never overlooks quiet obedience or faithful service done in love. Even when others do not notice, God sees hidden acts of faithfulness and honors them according to His wisdom and timing. The believer's motivation shifts from seeking recognition to trusting God, who remembers and values every act of obedience offered to Him.

Discussion Questions:

1. Read Hebrews 6:10. What does this verse reveal about God's character?

2. Why can hidden or unnoticed faithfulness sometimes feel discouraging?

3. According to Matthew 6:4, how does God respond to what is done in secret?

4. How does Psalm 18:25 encourage believers to trust God's faithfulness?

5. What would change if you fully believed that no act of obedience offered to God is ever wasted?

F. SECTION 3: PERSONAL APPLICATION & REFLECTION

1. Where do you most need to release hurry and trust God's timing more fully?

2. What does faithful obedience look like for you in this current season?

3. Which truth from today's discussion do you most need to carry with you this week?

4. What "small" area of faithfulness may God be asking you to continue without discouragement?

G. CLOSING WISDOM KEYS

1. God measures faithfulness by trustworthiness and steady obedience rather than visibility or speed.

2. Quiet faithfulness in small things forms the kind of character God can trust with greater responsibility.

3. Hope in Christ anchors believers through long seasons and sustains faithful endurance over time.

H. PRAYER

I. PRAYER POINTS

1. Ask God to strengthen your heart to remain faithful without comparison, hurry, or discouragement.

2. Pray for trust in God's timing and confidence that your obedience is never wasted.

3. Present your hidden burdens, responsibilities, and areas of weariness before God.

4. Ask the Holy Spirit to anchor your heart in hope and help you remain steady in ordinary faithfulness.

Ask for individual prayer requests and pray for the individual needs of your group members and any area the Spirit directs.

II. CLOSING PRAYER

Heavenly Father, thank You that You see and value every act of faithfulness offered to You in love. Help us release the pressure to prove ourselves or measure our lives by visible success. Teach us to remain steady, trustworthy, and hopeful even when the journey feels long or fruit seems delayed. Strengthen us to continue faithfully in small things and anchor our hearts in the hope that You are working according to Your perfect wisdom and timing. Thank You that nothing entrusted to You is ever wasted. In Jesus' name, Amen.

Use the Chapter 11 Daily Believer Declarations during the week.

KEY TRUTH TO REMEMBER

Faithfulness in God's Kingdom is measured by trustworthiness, sustained by hope, and rewarded by God over time—even when progress feels slow or unseen.

Daily Believer Declarations (Chapter 11)

The Secret of Faithfulness to the End

Day 1 — God Measures Faithfulness, Not Results

Scripture: 1 Corinthians 4:1–2

Declaration: I am a faithful steward of what God has entrusted to me.

Wisdom Key: God values trustworthiness more than visibility.

Prayer: Father God, help me live faithfully with what You have placed in my hands. Free me from measuring my life by results, and anchor me in what You value most. In Jesus' name. Amen.

Day 2 — God Rewards Faithfulness Over Time

Scripture: Matthew 25:21

Declaration: God sees my faithfulness and will reward it in His time.

Wisdom Key: What feels ordinary today matters deeply to God.

Prayer: Lord Jesus, when my obedience feels unnoticed, remind me that You see and remember. Help me remain faithful, trusting Your timing and Your reward. In Your name. Amen.

Day 3 — Faithfulness Under Pressure Is Not Wasted

Scripture: Hebrews 10:32–36

Declaration: My faithfulness under pressure is never wasted.

Wisdom Key: God honors obedience that continues even when the journey is hard.

Prayer: Father God, strengthen me to keep doing Your will when the pressure remains. Help me trust that my perseverance is meaningful to You. In Jesus' name. Amen.

Day 4 — Small Faithfulness Shapes Greater Trust

Scripture: Luke 16:10

Declaration: Faithfulness in small things is shaping my character for greater responsibility.

Wisdom Key: Small obedience forms a life God can trust.

Prayer: Abba Father, help me be faithful in the ordinary moments of today. Shape my heart through small acts of obedience that honor You. In Jesus' name. Amen.

Day 5 — God Remembers What Is Done in Secret

Scripture: Hebrews 6:10; Matthew 6:4

Declaration: God remembers and rewards what I do faithfully, even when it is unseen.

Wisdom Key: Hidden faithfulness is never hidden from God.

Prayer: Lord Jesus, thank You for seeing what others may never notice. Encourage my heart to keep serving faithfully with joy and trust. In Your name. Amen.

Day 6 — Hope Anchors My Faithfulness

Scripture: Hebrews 6:19; Romans 8:25

Declaration: Hope anchors my faithfulness and keeps me steady as I wait.

Wisdom Key: Hope frees faithfulness from hurry.

Prayer: Father God, anchor my heart in hope when waiting feels long. Help me trust You without rushing Your work in my life. In Jesus' name. Amen.

Day 7 — I Live with Hope, Not Hurry

Scripture: Galatians 6:9

Declaration: I remain faithful without hurry, trusting God's timing.

Wisdom Key: God's timing is purposeful and trustworthy.

Prayer: Father God, help me release pressure and remain faithful one step at a time. I trust that You are working even when I cannot see it. In Jesus' name. Amen.

Chapter 12 Study Guide: The Secret of Resurrection Hope

A. SESSION AIM

To help participants understand that the resurrection of Jesus guarantees future transformation, defeats death, and gives eternal meaning to present faithfulness—anchoring life in hope rather than fear, hurry, or discouragement.

B. ICE BREAKER

When you think about the word "forever," what feelings come to mind—comfort, peace, curiosity, uncertainty, or fear?

Leader Note: Keep this light and reflective. Encourage honest responses without trying to correct or "fix" them. The goal is to help participants begin thinking personally about eternity and hope.

C. OPEN YOUR SESSION WITH PRAYER

Invite someone to open in prayer, or use the prayer below:

Heavenly Father, thank You for the hope of resurrection through Jesus Christ. Anchor our hearts today in the assurance that death is defeated and that our lives have eternal meaning in You. Quiet fear, strengthen weary hearts, and help us live faithfully in light of forever. Guide our discussion with Your presence and truth. In Jesus' name, Amen.

D. INTRODUCTION (CHAPTER 12 SUMMARY)

There are seasons when faithfulness feels fragile and suffering feels heavy. Believers continue to trust, obey, and endure, yet quietly wonder whether any of it will matter in the end. Scripture answers that question with one of the greatest revelations in the Christian faith: because Jesus Christ rose from the dead, the story of God's people ends not in decay, defeat, or death—but in resurrection, transformation, and eternal life.

Resurrection hope is not vague optimism about life after death. It is the confident assurance that what is broken by the Fall will ultimately be restored through Christ. Bodies weakened by sickness, aging, and suffering will one day be transformed. Death itself—the last enemy—has already been defeated through the resurrection of Jesus.

This hope changes everything. It reframes suffering, steadies endurance, and gives eternal meaning to present obedience. Because Christ is risen, faithful labor is not wasted, suffering is not final, and fear no longer has the last word.

This chapter reminds us that resurrection hope is not only about the future—it reshapes how believers live courageously, faithfully, and steadily today.

E. BIBLE DISCUSSION

SECTION 1: PERSONALIZING THE MESSAGE

1. What fears or questions about the future most challenge your peace or hope sometimes?

2. Why do you think people often struggle with fear of death, loss, or uncertainty?

3. Have you ever experienced a season where eternal hope gave you strength during difficulty?

4. What area of your life currently needs greater resurrection hope?

SECTION 2: SCRIPTURE DISCOVERY

KEY POINT 1: Resurrection Promises Future Transformation

Scriptures: 1 Corinthians 15:51–53; Romans 8:18–23; 1 John 3:2

Scripture Insights: Scripture teaches that resurrection is not escape from the body but its redemption and transformation. Through Christ's resurrection, believers are promised future bodily renewal and eternal life. Present weakness, suffering, aging, and decay are temporary realities that will one day be overcome through God's final restoration.

Discussion Questions:

1. Read 1 Corinthians 15:51–53. What does Paul mean when he says "we will all be changed"?

2. Why is bodily transformation important to Christian hope?

3. According to Romans 8:18–23, what is creation itself waiting for?

4. How does 1 John 3:2 describe the believer's future hope?

5. How does resurrection hope speak into fear, weakness, sickness, or aging?

KEY POINT 2: Christ's Resurrection Defeated Death

Scriptures: 1 Corinthians 15:54–57; Romans 5:12; Hebrews 2:14–15

Scripture Insights: Scripture calls death the "last enemy," yet declares that through Jesus Christ death has been defeated. The resurrection of Jesus broke the power of sin, fear, and death over believers. Death remains real, but it is no longer ultimate. Because Christ lives, fear no longer has final authority over the believer's life.

Discussion Questions:

1. Why does Paul describe death as an "enemy" in 1 Corinthians 15:26?

2. What does it mean that death is "swallowed up in victory"?

3. According to Hebrews 2:14–15, what fear did Christ come to free people from?

4. How does Christ's resurrection change the way believers face death?

5. What fears lose power when resurrection hope becomes real in the heart?

KEY POINT 3: Resurrection Hope Anchors Believers Through Waiting and Suffering

Scriptures: Hebrews 6:19; Romans 8:25; 2 Corinthians 4:16–18

Scripture Insights: Biblical hope functions like an anchor that steadies believers through uncertainty, suffering, and delayed answers. Hope does not remove hardship immediately, but it keeps believers from drifting into despair or discouragement. Because resurrection guarantees God's final victory, believers can wait patiently and endure faithfully.

Discussion Questions:

1. Read Hebrews 6:19. How does the image of an anchor describe hope?

2. Why does Scripture connect hope with patient waiting?

3. According to 2 Corinthians 4:16–18, how does eternal perspective affect present suffering?

4. What pressures or disappointments most tempt believers to lose hope?

5. Where are you most tempted to hurry instead of trust God's timing?

KEY POINT 4: Resurrection Gives Eternal Meaning to Present Faithfulness

Scriptures: 1 Corinthians 15:58; Colossians 3:23–24; Matthew 25:21

Scripture Insights: Because Christ is risen, faithful labor is never wasted. Resurrection gives eternal significance to present obedience, service, sacrifice, and endurance. Believers can remain steady because what is done "in the Lord" carries lasting value beyond what is immediately visible.

Discussion Questions:

1. Read 1 Corinthians 15:58. What does the word "therefore" connect to in this verse?

2. How does resurrection make present obedience meaningful?

3. According to Colossians 3:23–24, who are believers ultimately serving?

4. Why can faithful labor sometimes feel unnoticed or discouraging?

5. What area of your faithfulness needs renewed hope and encouragement today?

KEY POINT 5: Resurrection Hope Reshapes How We Live Today

Scriptures: Colossians 3:1–2; Romans 8:25; 1 Corinthians 15:58

Scripture Insights: Resurrection hope is not only future-oriented—it transforms present living. Believers who live in light of eternity become steadier, more courageous, less fearful, less hurried, and more focused on what truly matters. Eternal perspective reshapes priorities, relationships, service, suffering, and daily decisions.

Discussion Questions:

1. Read Colossians 3:1–2. What does it mean to set your mind on things above?

2. How does believing in resurrection reshape daily priorities and decisions?

3. Why does eternal hope free believers from hurry and pressure?

4. In what ways can fear of loss quietly shape how people live?

5. What practical adjustment could help you live more intentionally "in light of forever"?

F. SECTION 3: PERSONAL APPLICATION & REFLECTION

1. What fear do you most need to surrender in light of resurrection hope?

2. Where do you need to stand firm instead of rushing ahead in anxiety or pressure?

3. What does "living in light of forever" practically look like in this season of your life?

4. What step of faithfulness is God inviting you to continue with renewed hope?

G. CLOSING WISDOM KEYS

1. Resurrection promises that weakness, suffering, and death are temporary realities—not the believer's final identity.

2. Because Christ defeated death, fear no longer has ultimate authority over believers.

3. Resurrection hope gives eternal meaning to present faithfulness and steadies believers for the long journey.

H. PRAYER

I. PRAYER POINTS

1. Ask God to anchor your heart more deeply in resurrection hope and eternal perspective.

2. Pray for freedom from fear of death, loss, uncertainty, or discouragement.

3. Present your present struggles, suffering, grief, or unanswered questions honestly before God.

4. Ask the Holy Spirit to help you remain faithful, courageous, and steady as you live in light of eternity.

Ask for individual prayer requests and pray for the individual needs of your group members and any area the Spirit directs.

II. CLOSING PRAYER

Heavenly Father, thank You that because Jesus Christ is risen, death is defeated and our future is secure in You. Thank You that suffering is not final, weakness is not permanent, and our labor in You is never wasted. Help us live with resurrection hope anchoring our hearts and shaping our daily lives. Free us from fear, hurry, and discouragement, and help us remain faithful, courageous, and steady as we wait for the fulfillment of Your promises. Thank You that the story of Your people ends not in death, but in eternal life with Christ forever. In Jesus' name, Amen.

Use the Chapter 12 Daily Believer Declarations during the week.

KEY TRUTH TO REMEMBER

The resurrection of Jesus guarantees future transformation, defeats death, and gives eternal meaning to present faithfulness—anchoring our lives in hope rather than fear or hurry.

The Secret of Resurrection Hope

Day 1 — My Future Is Secure

Scripture: 1 Corinthians 15:20; 1 Corinthians 15:22

Declaration: Because Christ is risen, my future resurrection is certain.

Wisdom Key: Resurrection hope is not wishful thinking — it is anchored in the risen Christ.

Prayer: Abba Father, thank You that my future is secure in Christ. Help me live today with confidence in the promise of resurrection life. In Jesus' name. Amen.

Day 2 — Death Is Not Final

Scripture: 1 Corinthians 15:26; 1 Corinthians 15:54

Declaration: Death is real, but it is not ultimate.

Wisdom Key: The last enemy has been defeated; fear no longer reigns over me.

Prayer: Lord Jesus, when fear whispers about endings, remind me that Christ has swallowed up death in victory. Steady my heart in resurrection hope. In Your mighty name. Amen.

Day 3 — My Life Is Not in Vain

Scripture: 1 Corinthians 15:58

Declaration: My life in the Lord is not empty or wasted.

Wisdom Key: Because Christ is risen, every act of faithfulness carries eternal weight.

Prayer: Father God, strengthen me to stand firm and serve faithfully, knowing my labor in You is not in vain. In Jesus' name. Amen.

Day 4 — My Identity Is Secured in Christ

Scripture: 2 Corinthians 5:17; Romans 4:25

Declaration: I am a new creation, forgiven and justified through the risen Christ.

Wisdom Key: Resurrection secures my identity and silences condemnation.

Prayer: Abba Father, help me live from the truth that I am made new in Christ. Free me from shame and anchor me in Your finished work. In Jesus' name. Amen.

Day 5 — Resurrection Power Is Active in Me Now

Scripture: Romans 6:4; Ephesians 1:19–20

Declaration: The same power that raised Jesus is at work in my life today.

Wisdom Key: Resurrection is not only future hope — it is present strength.

Prayer: Lord Jesus, empower me by Your Spirit to walk in newness of life. Let resurrection power shape my obedience today. In Your name. Amen.

Day 6 — Hope Anchors My Soul

Scripture: Hebrews 6:19; Romans 8:25

Declaration: Hope steadies me when the journey feels long.

Wisdom Key: Hope frees faithfulness from hurry and anchors my life in God's promises.

Prayer: Father, anchor my soul in hope. Help me wait patiently and trust Your timing. In Jesus' name. Amen.

Day 7 — I Live Today in Light of Forever

Scripture: Colossians 3:1–2; Revelation 21:4

Declaration: I live today with my eyes fixed on eternity.

Wisdom Key: Living in light of resurrection reshapes my priorities, courage, and joy.

Prayer: Father God, teach me to live in light of forever — steady, faithful, and courageous, knowing that Christ is risen and my future is secure. In Jesus' name. Amen.

Other Books

By

Mike Prah

HIDDEN NO MORE: THE SECRETS GOD REVEALS

What if the answers to life's deepest questions were never meant to stay hidden?

Hidden No More: The Secrets God Reveals explores the mysteries once hidden in God's redemptive plan but now revealed through Jesus Christ. Through twelve powerful biblical "secrets," Mike Prah shows how God's truth brings clarity, inspires transformation, strengthens faith in hardship, and anchors lasting hope for living with purpose and confidence.

The secrets are no longer hidden. Live in the light of what God has revealed.

Available in Hardcover, Paperback, E-Book, and Audio Book. Get your copy at:

http://mikeprah.com/bookstore

Also available at Amazon.com, BarnesandNobles.com, Books-a-Million, Walmart.com and several online bookstores, Audio books, and E-book retailers world-wide including Kindle, Apple Books, Google Books. For bulk purchases contact: info@mikeprah.com.

You Are Unstoppable. A 120-Day Devotional

Live with Purpose. Walk Boldly in Faith

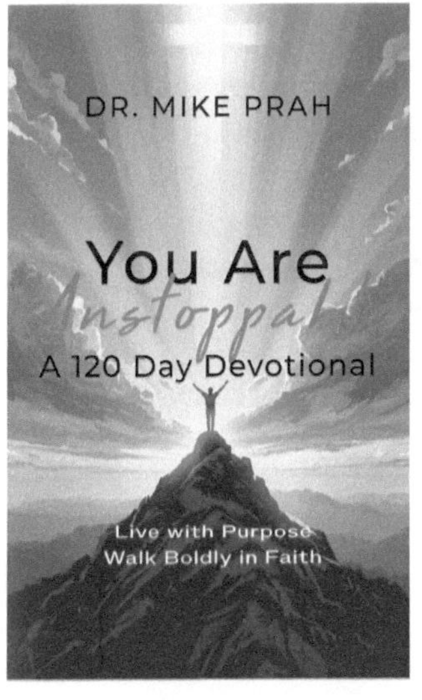

Whether you're facing a setback or embracing a new beginning, this devotional will help you draw from God's strength, live with purpose, and walk boldly in faith. With heartfelt prayers and reflection prompts, this 120-day journey will help you encounter God's presence in a powerful way.

You are not alone. You are not defeated. With God's help, *you are unstoppable.*

Available in Hardcover and Paperback at:

http://mikeprah.com/bookstore

Also available at Amazon.com, BarnesandNobles.com, Books-a-Million, Walmart.com and several online bookstores and E-book retailers world-wide. For bulk purchases contact: info@mikeprah.com.

YOU ARE UNSTOPPABLE: PRACTICAL PRINCIPLES FOR OVERCOMING SETBACKS AND EXPERIENCING BREAKTHROUGHS

DISCOVER HOW TO OVERCOME life's obstacles and step into your God-given destiny. In *You Are Unstoppable*, Mike Prah shares empowering biblical truths, inspiring stories, and practical strategies to help you experience breakthrough and live with purpose. Step into your calling—because with God, you are truly unstoppable!

Available in Hardcover, Paperback, E-Book, and Audio Book at

http://mikeprah.com/bookstore

Also available at Amazon.com, BarnesandNobles.com, Books-a-Million, Walmart.com and several online bookstores, Audio books, and E-book retailers world-wide including Kindle, Apple Books, Google Books. For bulk purchases contact: info@mikeprah.com.

You Are Unstoppable: Personal or Small Group Study Guide

Overcoming Setbacks. Experiencing Breakthroughs

This powerful 10-session companion to *You Are Unstoppable* is designed to help individuals and small groups apply life-changing biblical principles for breakthrough. With reflection prompts and discussion questions, Mike Prah equips you to turn setbacks into success and live with confidence, purpose, and freedom. You are truly unstoppable!

Available in Paperback from

http://mikeprah.com/bookstore

Also available at Amazon, BarnesandNobles, Books-a-Million and several online and E-book retailers world-wide. For bulk purchases contact: info@mikeprah.com

40 Days of Hope in Grief and Loss: A Devotional

If you're navigating the pain of grief, this 40-day devotional offers heartfelt encouragement through Scripture, real-life stories, and prayers. Mike Prah gently guides readers to find comfort, strength, and renewed hope in God's presence. Whether your loss is recent or long past, this book is a healing journey toward joy, purpose, and peace.

Available in Hardback from http://mikeprah.com/bookstore

Also available at Amazon.com, BarnesandNobles.com, Books-a-Million, Walmart.com and several online bookstores and E-book retailers world-wide.

For bulk purchases contact info@mikeprah.com

7 Secrets of Leaders Who Last

7 Secrets of Leaders Who Last equips pastors, ministry leaders, and servant-leaders to overcome the most common traps that derail leadership and embrace the habits that ensure longevity. Packed with a practical message outline, key takeaways, group discussion guide, and a 14-day devotional, this resource will help you to grow spiritually, lead effectively, and finish strong.

Whether you're leading a church, a ministry team, or a small group, this guide will inspire and equip you to serve with focus, humility, and endurance.

Available in Paperback from http://mikeprah.com/bookstore

Also available at Amazon.com, BarnesandNobles.com, Books-a-Million, Walmart.com and several online bookstores and E-book retailers world-wide. For bulk purchases contact: info@mikeprah.com

Skill Will Bring Success: Proven Principles for Living the Life of Your Dreams

Are you putting in the effort but not seeing results? It maybe time to sharpen your edge. Mike Prah unpacks biblical wisdom and real-life principles to help you develop the emotional, spiritual, and professional skills necessary for lasting success.

With clear teaching, practical tools, and a companion study guide, this book equips you to break through limitations, grow in wisdom, and live the life God intended for you. Skill will bring your success to life.

Available in Hardcover and Paperback at

http://mikeprah.com/bookstore

Also available at Amazon.com, BarnesandNobles.com, Books-a-Million, Walmart.com and several online bookstores, Audio books, and E-book retailers world-wide including Kindle, Apple Books, Google Books. For bulk purchases contact: info@mikeprah.com.

My Small Group Directory

NAME	PHONE NUMBER	E-MAIL

my notes

my notes

my notes

my notes

Most books authored by Mike Prah are available at special discounted rates for bulk purchases by churches, organizations, businesses, and individuals. Customized editions or book excerpts can also be created to meet the specific needs of your ministry, event, or audience. For more information or to inquire about a special order, please email info@mikeprah.com

Signed copies are also available from the author.